The Nocturnal Naturalist

THE NOCTURNAL NATURALIST

Exploring the Outdoors at Night

by Cathy Johnson

AN EAST WOODS BOOK

The Globe Pequot Press
Chester, Connecticut

Library of Congress Cataloging-in-Publication Data

Johnson, Cathy (Cathy A.)
    The nocturnal naturalist. — 1st ed.
        p. cm.
    Includes index.
    ISBN 0-87106-524-X
    1. Nature. 2. Night. 3. Seasons. I. Title.
QH81.J6 1989
508—dc20   89-7549
                                             CIP

Manufactured in the United States of America
First Edition/First Printing

To Harris, who is there for me like the moon at midnight; to Mary, who gave me the nights to discover; to Ann, who encourages always.

Contents

About the Author

Cathy Johnson is a naturalist, artist, and writer with a keen interest in our natural environment. She is a member of the Audubon Society, Wilderness Society, National Wildlife Federation, and Greenpeace; in 1987 she was chosen the Conservation Communicator of the Year by Burroughs Audubon Society.

Cathy has authored eight books on the subjects of art and nature. She writes and illustrates a quarterly natural-history column in *Country Living* magazine. She also writes for *The Artist's Magazine,* contributing a regular monthly column in addition to other articles. Cathy is originally from Independence, Missouri; she now resides in Excelsior Springs.

Foreword

Cathy Johnson is the most important kind of explorer: an explorer of the everyday or, in the case of this book, of the "everynight." For her, discovery comes not when a mountaintop is reached or an ocean depth is plumbed, but whenever the sun sets, the moon rises, a maple tree loses its leaves, or a particularly loud species of katydid sings in her garden. This kind of exploration is more important than the kind that newspaper headlines feature because it nourishes an attitude toward life on earth that is needed badly.

When people perceive their everyday surroundings as ordinary and dull, it becomes easier for them to exploit or destroy those surroundings through pollution or overdevelopment. If, on the other hand, they find in their surroundings an endless source of amusement, allure, and learning, they are more likely to resist its destruction. Few people can be mountain climbers or deep-sea divers, much less astronauts; but almost everyone, from Montana ranchers to New York highrise dwellers, can make daily discoveries in the diversity and complexity of nature, in its stars, clouds, rocks, plants, and animals. That they may not be the first ones to make such discoveries is unimportant; what is important is that people should continue to discover for themselves. Fortunately, curiosity and wonder seem to be innate in human beings. The more people can develop these qualities, the better will be the prospects that the earth can remain the wonderful, curious place it is.

Cathy Johnson is an important explorer also because she communicates her findings gracefully with words and drawings. In its wry, unpretentious way, The Nocturnal Naturalist is as full of adventure and spectacle as a polar journal. Johnson has an explorer's fascination for other forms of life, so her small-town Missouri house has opossums in the basement, crickets under the bed, raccoons in the yard, owls in the shrubbery, and flying squirrels in the bird feeder. Excursions to Ozark lakes, Missouri woodlands, and a Nevada desert bring other close encounters of the earthly kind.

As the book moves through an "everynight" year, each change of weather and season brings a new cast of characters. Spotted salamanders throng the woods on the first night of late-winter warm rains. Mysterious insects rustle the dry leaves of early spring. A black snake goes hunting birds' eggs in the lush treetops of early summer. A brown spider builds a web with 756 "stitches" in a September garden. A barred owl pursues a great blue heron through December woods.

Johnson is sensitive not only to the other life that surrounds her, but to the cosmic and meteorological phenomena on which life depends: the movements of stars and meteors, the fluctuations of air masses and humidity, and, perhaps most of all, the rise and set of sun and moon, which she observes and describes with never-failing appreciation. She not only observes, she experiments. She hangs a prism in a November moonbeam and discovers that it, too, casts a spectrum: "Dancing on the white folds of my nightgown, the dusky nightbow moves with my outstretched hand. The colors are subtle, muted. I see more rusty reds and purples and maroons and siennas than daylight's blues and greens and oranges. But there it is, nonetheless. A nightbow on my lap, a caught prize, magical and moving." Catching a nightbow seems to me the essence of Johnson's discoveries — familiar and accessible, yet unexpected and profound.

Like all successful explorers, Johnson brings a wide knowledge to her observations and experiments. She knows that apparently cold and colorless moonbeams carry enough red light to permit the taking of photographs at night, photographs that "are as colorful as sun shots, if the film is sufficiently exposed." Her writing is full of informed reflections on subjects as various as the nature of down comforters, the making of compost, the anatomy of the eye, and the formation of frost.

The Nocturnal Naturalist contains ample evidence that Cathy Johnson is a committed, passionate defender of the place she knows so well. Because of her, the woods near her house are a state natural area, their plants and animals protected from thoughtless destruction. To anyone who wants to follow in her path, which is the path of survival, this book will be a guide.

DAVID RAINS WALLACE

Preface

The night is a strange country to most of us. Diurnal creatures by nature, we stumble around in the dark as if blinded. Our eyes are made for depth and color, not for the dim monochrome of night. We are at a disadvantage. The humblest house cat far outstrips us in the ability to see, to navigate, in the dark. We are unequivocally creatures of the day, suited to its hours. We know them. They are as familiar to us as our own faces in the mirror. But if we are willing to try the night, its rewards are great.

The night is not a time to fear but to welcome. It has its own unique gestalt to offer if we can set aside our prejudice. There is mystery and adventure here; ask any kid who explores the chimerical world he knows so well by day.

The frontiers of night, naturally beguiling, draw us beyond their borders. Sunset sends its long arrows of light to pierce us to the heart. We wish it would last forever — or just, please, just one more moment. Sunrise is as magical. Clouds that glow with foxfire lights may disappear completely in the heat of a full-summer morning.

Yet maybe it takes an insomniac naturalist to enjoy the quest for night itself, to peer through its shadows, to search down its dark hours on a pilgrimage of discovery. If so, I am that insomniac, exploring an unknown country. Thoreau had his Walden, Darwin his Galápagos. If I have the hours from dusk to dawn, I am satisfied.

Unlike the known and crowded daylight, there is still much to be unearthed from these strange hours, and with a freedom not possible by day. If one is willing to adapt, the darkness offers a place to step beyond the known edge and explore, a place of silence and sound, a place both unpopulated and populous, filled with things we may not see by day. I collect them like a bowerbird and offer them as gift.

Acknowledgments

No one writes a book like this without help. Field guides and texts are invaluable, of course, but beyond that we need specific and personal answers (the human touch) for our questions.

When I needed help, my telephone was always close at hand. After all, only a dial tone away were experts like: Joe Werner, urban biologist for the Conservation Commission of the state of Missouri; John Wylie, now retired from the commission but still and always ready to help; Joe Francka, entomologist for the Missouri Department of Agriculture; Mac Johnson, editor of the *Missouri Conservationist*; John Schutz, M.D., always willing to answer my questions about adrenalin and such; Fred Ostby, at the National Severe Storms Forecast Center; and Burt Wagenknecht, biologist at William Jewell College in Liberty, Missouri.

Friends and neighbors were generous with questions, experiences, and wonders, especially Wendy McDougal, H. A. Dickey, and my ever helpful veterinarians, Ed Piepergerdes, Pete Rucker, and Vinson Rucker. Ann Zwinger provided guidance and moral support when the nights seemed altogether *too* long.

Mary Kennan started this book on its way; Bruce Markot guided it into safe harbor — where would a writer be without good editors? And the good people at The Globe Pequot Press, from copy editor to designer, from art director to president, all have my gratitude for their support.

My deepest appreciation goes to David Rains Wallace, fellow writer, fellow wanderer in the night, for his lovely Foreword.

Special thanks (but thanks are not enough, not by a long shot) go to Patti Delano, who read and encouraged and kept me laughing.

And there always was my dear Harris. Without him none of this would work. It would *happen*, but it wouldn't work.

Introduction

This book is organized neither by month nor by arbitrary quarters. Spring, summer, fall, and winter are not so easily delineated. There is Blackberry Winter. There is Indian Summer. If we do not keep one eye on the calendar, we are liable to mistake the January thaw for spring. Here in the Midwest, and indeed anyplace in the United States where frost reaches its cold fingers deep into the earth, there is also Mud Season. Muck time — when the frost goes out. Spring thaw.

At night, frost firms the earth, and we can walk where, by the light of day, we would have sunk in mud up to our knees. It is one of the good gifts of the night. Mud time comes in January in some parts of the country, February or March in others. Here in Missouri it is coy; it comes and goes and comes again until spring, true spring, sets its boundaries and the mud dries up. And so the seasons will not be neatly delineated, sliced off and catalogued into fourths.

In this book, you will find short chapters and longer ones. They reflect the quicksilver nature of the night, the turning of the earth, and the immense passing of weather fronts. If early autumn seems short, it is because it *is* — over all too quickly, ephemeral as a spring shower. If full summer seems to stretch on forever, so does the season reflected. There is more to see in these long, warm stretches; nature is never more active, at least visibly so.

The book was kept as an ongoing night journal marking nature's moments, large and small. If in the stretch of summer or the endless ice-locked nights of midwinter it seemed that nothing much changed from night to night, I picked up happenings from my journals of other years. They were of the same season, the same date, but with their own unique soundings to be marked.

Each chapter has its introduction, a hint of the season and its characteristic occurrences: a bit of the flavor we expect. Animals we may see, migrating birds usual at this time, a mention of the meteor showers that take place in each month — it is a haphazard summing up that evokes a mood if not a particularity. Individual journal entries take care of the latter.

This book, then, is a record, a naturalist's field journal of my findings on the frontier of night. My observations were made on the spot; the questions they raised were researched by the light of day so that the questions and their answers formed the hours of this nightbook. It's as good a measure of a life as any other.

SPRING

The Tenderest Months

SPRING HAS BEEN A LONG TIME COMING. Like anything longed for and anticipated, it seemed never to move closer. Or it came in schizoid fits and starts, unwilling or unable to commit itself to change. This stop-and-go reluctance was more true at night than in the warmer daylight hours. Then, spring's hints became flat statements of an obvious truth; only an idiot could have misinterpreted them. But at night winter returned with a circadian as well as a seasonal rhythm. It seemed as if these small repeated winters would never pass.

March has been called the cruelest month, and not only for the frozen buds and too-early nesting of birds that a return of cold may kill. Our own hopes have been raised. We have laid spring plans, we have planted and tilled. We have believed the promise only to find our premature expectations in tatters at our feet. There is a certain blowy uncertainty that is as much mood as weather.

But still spring does make its immense seasonal stand. Like a rock-climber, it finds a toehold and hangs on, however tenuously. The thirty-five-degree isotherm retreats northward with the winter, as spring pushes its way up the continent, tender and inexorable. It comes at last, and it is welcomed with a fanfare of wildflowers waving in a March wind, of wild trumpet voices of migrating geese, of cymbal-throated frogs in every pond in the land. Like the images in a medieval tapestry, spring is all flowers and song and the elusive scent of unicorns in the wood.

The changes come too fast to track once they have fully begun. After winter's slow time-lapse changes, spring is set in fast forward. One year I vowed to paint each flower as it bloomed in April woods; I foundered after six. They came and went like strobe-lit images. At night it is no different.

For a time it seems as if spring peepers fill every cubic foot with sound, packing it dense and squirming. The escalating crescendo that emanates from the tiny, vibrating throats fills my eardrums to bursting, a sensation both exquisitely painful and sharply pleasurable. I wonder if I cannot stand the joy of it another moment. Then, all too quickly, the tiny three-quarter-inch frogs clam up, cease their mating calls, lay their eggs, and make their way back to the anonymous woods.

Spring is a time of firsts, a time to enumerate change. Impossible though it may be, the desire to track and note and mark each spinning change of winter into spring is irresistible. It is in our blood. There is the first pale wildflower glowing like a lit candle in the dawn; the first migrant robin singing his descant song long after sunset fades; the first arias of the dawn chorus, suddenly, subtly different from winter's more businesslike birdsong: It is unmistakable.

The return of insects to the night may be the surest sign of all. On a warm winter day we may find snow fleas like spilled pepper on a sunny slope, but the night is still and silent. Now there are small, chitinous wings battering softly at our lighted windows and haloing street lights with a moving aura. I feel their breathlike flutter against a bare shoulder, and I shudder down the length of my spine like a touched mare.

The sky itself may be lit with change. When winter wears thin, and the earth begins to kick back on its axis, we may find the small, familiar sky wrapped in the shimmering veils of the Northern Lights, a magnetic phenomenon that paints the firmament with silent, moving color.

It is a fickle season, changeable, quicksilver. Tender days and tender nights are suddenly locked away again behind jailhouse doors of ice. The towering change of a weather front may bring devastation. We hear the sounds of tornado sirens at the lee edge of night and hope *this* change passes us by. Sometimes it does not, and trees and homes blow flat. Most times it is only sound and fury signifying spring.

MARCH 1 • *Early*

Blood-red buds swell and burst with antic gold stamens on the Norway maple; the sap is rising in the trees. They feel the spring as I do, cold, thin, shivering in its shoes, but coming nonetheless.

Overnight, the sap that filled a hollow in the big maple overflowed and froze in a long, amber stalactite. It must be sap oozing out over itself and freezing, imperceptibly, solid. It is too high to reach, but from the ground it looks as long as a gargoyle's tooth, at least eighteen inches. By midmorning it will melt, and only an acid green wetness down the algae-painted bark will tell me it was there.

Last night we took a winding walk up the hill at sunset, and, under a bit of dried fungus on the ground, I found the first ladybug of spring.

This bright little paint drop of a beetle had just emerged from hibernation under the leaf litter, where she has huddled in concert with hundreds of her kind. One winter when we lived on the farm, I uncovered a great mound of them, as if someone had dropped a bucket of scarlet pigment, then covered the evidence with dead leaves.

One fall I caught the first of the ladybird beetles as they moved in a multicolored mass into winter hiding. I have yet to find a lay person who will believe me. It was a magical sight, a one-to-a-customer thrill—you had to be there. There were the common red ladybugs. There were also ashy gray ones with black spots, black ones with red spots, golden ones with black spots, red ones with no spots, and even a rather avocado green model. It was years later when I came across my vindication in a book: there *are* many kinds and colors—and styles—of ladybugs.

Last night there was only one tiny ladybug, still looking for her children, perhaps, as the old rhyme goes,

> *"Ladybug, ladybug, fly away home;*
>
> *Your house is on fire*
>
> *and your children will burn..."*

Another bloodthirsty unexamined childhood rhyme!

It feels as if spring must be here already, though the calendar insists on three more weeks of winter. The tiny crocuses by the back door have opened, purple and white and bright butter yellow, keyed to the lengthening days. But winter it is. I will not count my ladybugs — not just yet.

MARCH 2 • *Sunset*

There is change in the air. I swear I can feel the earth tilt back to the south.

The sky is still translucent blue overhead with a stain of orange ringing the setting sun. Against that bright sky the earth seems little more than a silhouette, one cut fine with small, sharp scissors, like a folk-art *scherenschnitt*. The limbs of bare trees are suddenly fancy with buds. The box-elder tree is full of late-dining starlings daintily plucking buds with exaggerated care, sampling the hors d'oeuvres one by one like society ladies. They are only black shapes. I cannot see their glossy, oiled iridescence or pink legs. I cannot tell their fine bills are a bright breeding yellow. But I can see that distinctive starling shape—the blackbird family physique—and the Elizabethan ruff of neck feathers.

Minutes later, when I look, the sun is gone and so are the starlings, as if sucked to the west after the sun, where they still seek winter's communal roosts.

MARCH 3 · *Night*

Great, moving curtains of light undulate across the sky like blown grasses on the prairie. Can it be the Northern Lights? They appear even this far south as winter wears thin and spring pokes through the bare spots. The auroras are high-altitude phenomena, actions of a harsh and changeable exosphere some 350 to 600 miles up. Ions of gas at this level are battered mercilessly by cosmic rays, blown to atoms in earth's thin pneumon. The Northern Lights are the product of streams of solar particles, far from home, acting on the ionosphere at these altitudes. They appear most often at the poles, where the earth's magnetism draws the particles down to glow in neon curtains in the night sky.

But no, it is not such a midcontinental rarity after all. Looking toward the moon back over my shoulder, I see my "lights" are only thin clouds skittering out of the south, so thin they are powerless to mask the moon. They caught fire in the west with the lights of town and masquerade as aurora borealis.

MARCH 4 · *Night*

There are strange happenings in the darkness, strange bits of light in the sky. They glow so brightly, so steadily. What can they be? Anxious sky watchers call in to the late news to ask. Is it a saucer, a pair of them? They cannot be planes; they hover too steadily, moving almost imperceptibly to the western horizon.

It is funny what imagination stirs behind such unaccustomed eyes. We are so unused to watching the night sky we can scarcely find the Dipper, the drinking gourd that a hundred years ago guided the slaves through Missouri's underground railroad to safety in the north or to free state Kansas. We have become so divorced from the natural world —divorced and scarcely granted visiting rights—that these strange lights

have people alarmed, ill at ease. We expect the worst; H. G. Wells may
have had something there.

I had to laugh when the weatherman reported the calls—after a
quick check, that is, of my *own* slice of sky. It was only bright Venus and
Jupiter in their March alignment, brilliant and side by side, just offset
near the horizon.

MARCH 5 • *Night*

The full moon of March has more names than it can handle. A nineteenth
century book of natural history happenings, *Nature's Program*, calls it the
Wakening or Crow Moon; this year's *Old Farmer's Almanac* calls it the Sap
Moon.

The Wakening Moon and the Sap Moon fit like two mittens knit just
for the wearer. March is a month of wakening. Buds fatten on the trees
as the sap rises. They stand out like rough knots against the sunset; I
notice them especially in that warm-tinted brilliance. Bees awaken to
find a fringe of pollen-dusted stamens at each bud and the thin sweetness within. At night the first of the moths look avidly for sustenance;
perhaps they find it in the nectar of tree buds as well. Each dawn seems
to bring something new, just visible above the still-cold ground, as if
things grew in furtive darkness. This early, though, it is mostly our
hardy domestic bulbs rather than nature's greenery. In the swamp by
Fishing River I may follow the nose-tickling, fetid odor to skunk cabbage, usually the first to poke its folded green hood above the ground.

The Wakening Moon shines on the reawakening of territorial concerns; casual feeding flocks, which traveled like small Gypsy bands all
winter, now split up to stake their claims. Cardinals and titmice are not
the only dawn singers to change their winter tune. The chorus grows as
birds proclaim their overlapping, arbitrary property lines. There is a new
sound to their calls; it is near arrogant and proprietary. The best singers
claim the land and with it, a mate.

It is that mating and brood raising that has given the name to the
Crow Moon. Silent as a nesting crow, the moon watches through the
bare branches. Migrant crows have returned to stake out their small
holdings among the birds that wintered over. They have broken their
loose flocks into family groups. A nesting pair and last year's young
keep company still, with the older siblings overseeing the nest. These
normally raucous birds are now sly and secretive; no one should know

where they nest—and with good cause. They are none too popular with most humans, nor with other birds who resent and fear these pushy, loudmouthed neighbors. But to protect their young the crows become uncharacteristically silent. Why draw the attention of enemies?

MARCH 6 · *Night*

On this warm, wet night one of nature's grand events is unfolding, prearranged from time's dawning. Herpetologists have waited all year for this one night—the night of the first warm rain. The date does not matter. There could be patches of snow on the ground and flourishes of ice at the edges of deserted ponds. If the rain falls warm, spotted salamanders will come out from winter's hiding under the duff and fallen logs and make for the nearest open water to mate and lay their eggs.

Small, fleshy, handlike, their tiny feet push aside the leaf litter to emerge almost blindly, driven by powerful instinct. They arrow in from all directions, unerringly making their way to the one thing they need to complete their life cycles: water.

Hundreds of these small nocturnal amphibians will converge on a single fishless pond; you can scarcely avoid stepping on them. They need to choose wisely; the pond *must* be fishless or their thick, gelatinous streamers of eggs will be devoured, and their great night's work destroyed.

Awakening, migration to water, mating, egg laying—it is all over in one turning of the clock, and it is hidden in darkness. By full daylight the salamanders will have crawled away again to hide in the leaf litter. If we are lucky, indeed, we may find one there under a fallen log; most people never see them.

John Wylie, natural history officer for the Missouri Department of Conservation, alerted me to this salamander assignation. I never would have guessed the woods were alive and moving out this first warm, wet night. Near the peeper pond on the hill I find the dance is on. Slick, soft sides glisten in the dark as the salamanders pull themselves forward. Their skin wrinkles alternately along each side as they snake along toward the fine, pale glow of the water. Their chill fleshiness is strange to warm-blooded creatures, as if the mud itself had come to life in midnight alchemy and crawled inexorably to ponds and lakes and bogs. I can feel their determination—or imagine I can—and their urgency. They will not be deterred. I step in front of one, and it detours. I nudge one, and it shrugs off my touch. I pick one up, and it squirms wildly, demanding freedom. I oblige—who can stand in the way?

Finally, I sit quietly, wrapped in my poncho, and float in a moving river of salamanders. It is as if the ground itself stirs, parts around me, and passes on.

MARCH 7 · *Night*

There is a kind of texture to the darkness, a substance, a heft. It has rained and drizzled and rained again, late afternoon into evening. At last. It has been dry too long. Now, at 10:00 P.M., the darkness is almost tactile. The quiet is woven with the sounds of dogs. I hear them call from neighborhood to neighborhood in their varied voices. A random non-rhythm directs the sounds, a chaotic symphony of small-town Saturday night.

I hear cars out on the highway, singly or in convoys, heading for the city—heading anywhere but this backwater bedroom community, twenty-eight miles from Kansas City.

Let them go. Let them all go. When they are gone, the sound of cars and trucks will be reeled in behind them, leaving silence. Wonderful silence, woven with dog's voices and the syncopated plop and spatter of moisture that has gathered on tree limbs to roll in silver mercury drops to the ground.

MARCH 8 · *Predawn*

An early morning ride into the delicate world of hoarfrost; visual winter still surrounds us. It could scarcely look more cold and frozen, barren as January in the weak gray light.

A raccoon—the biggest I have ever seen, big as a bear cub—ambles arrogantly along the side of the road as if he held title to the thoroughfare. After a night's feeding, he wanders back to his den, apparently too stuffed to do more than waddle. He was coming from an old farm, one with a wooden corncrib. I suspect he found it to his liking and far easier to scale than galvanized metal.

It *looks* like winter still, until we notice the silhouettes of the trees against the lightening sky. Transparent, bare limbs only last week, some are now already on their way to becoming opaque with deep maroon buds. And as the light gathers I can see willows along the creek, their twigs glowing that tender yellow-green of early spring as if the rising sap fluoresces beneath the thin skin of bark. Beyond the creek at the edge of the woods, there are twigs that blush reddish; early spring hints at fall colors, as if it cannot wait for color of its own.

And if I need further proof of the coming season, there is a bluebird,

calm as the Mona Lisa, *posing* on the barbed-wire fence. Its back is the lovely sky color of the dawn. Its breast matches the blush of the twigs, the glow in the east.

There is another. And another! There are four bluebirds within a single mile on this small gravel road, and my heart is inexplicably light as if filled, suddenly, with helium. I am not driving, I am flying, gliding, *soaring*.

Around the bend past the long hill, where a tiny unnamed brook bisects the valley, a flock of red-winged blackbirds confirms the reservation made by the single bird we saw at Rocky Hollow last week. They wear the rising sun on their flashing epaulets.

It is as if we drove from winter to early spring in the space of a single dawn.

MARCH 9 • *Dawn*

A solitary robin—the first to return to my territory, our shared domain—repeats his descending-note sequence, his spring song, as distinctive as a fingerprint. A long winter may have passed without hearing from him, but I know the voice of an old friend.

MARCH 10 • *Night*

The turning of the year is contained in the fragile wings of insects. Spring may be two weeks away by the calendar, but it has arrived at my front porch light.

Every week for four weeks, I have left the porch light on for a while to see if it might finally attract signs of vernal nightlife. There are signals in plenty in the daytime now, from the sturdy daggers of jonquils and tulips and the delicate crocuses to the robins' parceling off of our lots into territories of their own. But night is reluctant to make its move. Its intimations of spring are more likely to occur at dusk or dawn, unless you are able to read the turning of the seasons in the skies. The Big Dipper has moved out of the extreme north and has migrated southward before the first of the birds, bringing the whole of the night sky with it, a calendar of days made up of glittering points of light.

I have heard the barred owls mating on the hill and known by their cacophony that spring was waiting in the chilly wings for its cue. And I have seen two tiny nightmoths in the woods, mysterious light shapes against the darkness. They did not wait to make my acquaintance. They never stopped to chat. They simply whispered of spring.

Now I believe the rumor. Right here, by the webby light on my winter-dusty porch, before my nearsighted eyes and close enough to touch—life. Spring. For a tactile person, whose fingers often believe more than her eyes, it is proof positive and more tangible than a tide of salamanders. I feel the delicate touch of wings on my bare arm, a flutter against my cheek: seven mosquitolike midges, a dun-colored moth with back-folded wings, two small flying insects like precursors of oak lace bugs. Spring is contained in the wings of insects.

MARCH 11 • *Night*

My muscles ache from the unaccustomed activity, and my hands are paper dry from the soil, but I feel only a sense of profound satisfaction, bone deep. The new garden is tilled and marked off with stakes and rope to protect it from careless feet. The peas and lettuce and spinach are in. I stand by its shrinking perimeters. It looked so big before rows were scribed into its blank surface. I inhale the sweet scent of freshly turned soil. Even now, long after dark when the temperature has dropped below freezing, I can smell that sweet earth scent, the scent of microscopic organisms that populate the loam.

Who knows what this first garden will bring? The land was backyard for decades before the house next door burned. Who can imagine the capabilities of soil hidden beneath brick and sod? What does the earth hold within itself? The topsoil was purchased to fill the hole where the house had been. Here and there I can just discern the ghostly gleam of limestone foundation rocks unearthed by the tiller. They glow with less intensity than those streaks of white rope that delineate the small plot of possibilities we planted here.

It is a cooperative venture. Harris and I are hardly alone. We will work hand in hand with the mysteries contained in a seed, with the turning of the earth on its seasonal axis, with the stars and sun and rain, with the earth itself. We till and seed and water only; the real work is done by older forces.

MARCH 12 • *10:30 P.M.*

Changes come almost too quickly to assimilate. They spin by before my eyes in doubletime, and I have that half-sad, half-panicky feeling that I am missing most of the show by being in one place and not another, in one place and not a *thousand* others.

We rode into the country to enjoy the balmy night. Weathermen are calling for rain and snow over the weekend and we seize the moment with both hands, greedy as kids upon the breaking of a piñata.

We got more than our share. The dark moonless night was perfect for a ride over the roller coaster hills north of town. We kept our windows down to smell the changed scent of waning winter in forty-five-degree country air. We sniffed like bears coming out of hibernation. No town smells here, no car exhaust, no gas, no fried food from fast-food joints, just the pervasive earth-scent of thawing soil, new growth, newly melted ponds.

These high-ground ponds caught and held our attention; how could they do otherwise? We heard their auditory signals a quarter of a mile away and more. I knew the sweet sound instantly: spring peepers.

These tiniest of chorus frogs are the earliest to sing here in Missouri, all crawling out at once from muddy hibernation. They are jubilant as sleigh bell at their sudden freedom. One tiny frog sounds like many, not only in his astonishing volume—*impossible* coming from that thumbnail-sized body, that miniscule, vibrating throat—but by a kind of trick of the notes themselves. They seem to overlap, weave in on themselves, magnify themselves. Little wonder; the best singer mates most often.

I turn off the car's engine just upslope from one of these noisy farm ponds, douse the lights, ease off the brake and sink into sound. They are very cautious little creatures. Approach too boldly, too noisily, and they clam up. The silent, sliding car is the perfect vehicle to infiltrate the wall of noise. Only the crunch of gravel under the tires gives us away, enough to alert a number of the tiny singers. The decibel level drops by half for a minute or two until we stop fully and sit silently just level with the water. It glows oddly incandescent in the darkness. There is no moon to light it, only the collected candlepower of the stars.

We wait, silent as stones, and after a bit the full chorus resumes, *a cappella*. I could not have been more enthralled by the Vienna Choir Boys. The voices are as high and as sweet, but with that fine, lovely distinction of being *other*. Not us. Not human. Wild.

MARCH 13 • *Night*

I had not seen Old Silver, the Virginia opossum, in weeks. I wondered if he had gone elsewhere, found a den off in the woods. The basement had been silent, and I missed the comfortable snuffling, the soft sounds of his coming and going.

But today I put out some chicken livers that were just that much too old to cook. Apparently our fine-haired felines thought so, too. Even wild Cougar turned them down flat. As I stepped out into the darkness I scared Old Silver off from his find: chicken liver carrion *al fresco*. It suited him just fine, and he did not go far, only ducked under the porch to wait impatiently for me to leave. Not much is wasted around here, even rotten chicken livers.

A bit later, I take my penlight to the back door to see if he has returned to finish the livers. He has, and with him is a friend. I had thought Old Silver was a large opossum—perhaps his light color made him seem so—but this darker possum is a behemoth. His fur is slightly curly, a dirty gray with a silver underfur. He is concentrating hard on dispatching the livers, one by one. He picks one up in his front paws and sits back on his fat haunches to devour the slippery mass. I watch as he clutches it with one paw, nearly drops it, then grabs tightly with both. It disappears down his gullet, chomped to bits with sharp white teeth.

Old Silver has finished his share, but now I see why the plate is always polished by morning. He works it over methodically, washing it with a long, pink tongue. It looks like an anteater's tongue flickering in and out from that long silver snout. But it is efficient. There is not a speck of food left on the plate when he is finished.

As we ready ourselves for bed, I hear a familiar sound multiplied by two: the water pipes bang in the basement, as not one, but two opossums find their way to its warmth, squeezing between the pipes. And I realize how much I had missed that sound, inexplicably—wildlife in the basement. Where had they been?

MARCH 14 • *Sunset*

We imagine ourselves to be owners of the earth, by divine right as well as in our small plots by authority of law and by hard cash. But we are only an accretion living on the surface or layered somewhere in between an older authority.

Charles Gusewelle, author and columnist for the *Kansas City Star*, writes of a gang of crows, an "empire" of crows "in numbers usually associated with starlings on the move. But these were crows, unmistakable by the way they paddled with slow oar strokes across the still lake of the softening afternoon."

The birds filled the sky over the commuting automobiles, clouds of them, southbound in mingling, braided groups. Crows form migrating bands in the fall, not in the spring. In spring they normally return in family groups.

And what was really amazing in Gusewelle's sighting of the thousands of crows was that they seemed to come to a stopping place, an invisible wall where they turned back upon themselves and wove back through the cloud of south-flying birds without missing a beat. What had turned them back? Why did they decide on this odd aerial choreography, backpedaling through the air as if by mutual agreement? It all took place in mystery, unnoticed by the homeward-bound commuters.

MARCH 15 • *Predawn*

There is an odd sound in the basement. Is there something wrong with the furnace? I open the basement door to listen, but the sound is softer from here. Like a hound hunting by sound alone, I follow my ears to the loudest point—the bathroom.

The sound buzzes up through the floor joists, the decibel level highest just by the furnace vent. It is a continuous broken bubbling—a snore, I realize with amusement. It is Old Silver, out like a stone after a hard night. The sound is amplified by the metal furnace pipe he sleeps on for warmth.

MARCH 16 • *Predawn*

Our lovely blackberry winter is over. The warm days and temperate nights lured us outdoors for long hours, pulled wool over our eyes, lied to us, bald-faced. Though spring—by the calendar—is only a week away, winter feels as strong as January. During the night the temperature hovered around seventeen degrees. With the wind chill it feels like zero this morning and cuts my jacket to shreds.

I planted strawberries during blackberry winter's sweet blandishments. I listened to the lies and now the tiny new leaves look pale and frosted against the ice-hard earth. They are folded in on themselves to conserve warmth, showing their light backsides.

Sap rose again in the Norway maple overnight. The sap is icicle shaped, nearly three feet long and golden as syrup. It looks pale in this dim light, and it reminds me of an old syrup maker's trick to concentrate sweetness. It takes long hours to boil down sap for syrup, as well as prodigious amounts of wood. It is possible to hurry the process along by freezing the sap first to separate out at least a part of the water. If I could reach the long icicle of sap, I would taste it to see if it were as sweet as it looks.

MARCH 17 • *Dusk*

There is no sunset, just a gradual darkening, a dimming, a grim, gray dusk. I feel as though I am going blind.

How quickly I got used to that false spring. It felt like home. My flowers felt it, and the birds. A paper wasp was busy at the never-ending task of turning the wooden fence into wasp's nest with his tiny buzz saw mandibles. Bees tumbled among the crocus. At night the moths fluttered at street lights and at my lighted windows. Blackberry winter lulls us all into false starts, then calls us back with a raucous alarm.

Now, this hard metallic cold is miserable, like a betrayal. I hate it. I do not like going backwards. I hate false starts. Perhaps March *is* the cruelest month, after all.

MARCH 18 • *2:30 A.M.*

Icy sparkles of light fall from the unbroken clouds. I look up to watch their falling, drifting like a cone around my shoulders. I could not see a moon if there were one—nothing but this glittering dark.

In the deep cold before dawn the flakes were thick and individual, spacial dendrites with a heavy accretion of frostlike coating. They looked *too* white and artificial, as though cut from polystyrene plastic. They were oversized like the man-made flakes in a domed plastic snow scene from my childhood. I could cause a blizzard by picking up the small world and upending it. It snowed all day long. Wet clumps and graupel and drifting single flakes fell on warming ground, melting.

Now, long after dark, the flakes continue to fall with the mercury. The ground is cold enough again to preserve them, and they begin to build up like a dusting of sugar. They form fine ice webs between them like ephemeral mycelium and fall in concert to coat the wet twigs and buds and blades of grass. The fattening buds look fatter still with sticky new snow to decorate them. They almost make me believe they have bloomed with a million delicate white flowers.

In three more days it will be spring. I am as anxious as a kid on Christmas Eve. I had a taste. It whetted my appetite. And now this cold, white winter holds little appeal. I am done with it. Let's get on with it. Bring on the flowers and birds and miniature, squirming tadpoles.

MARCH 19 • *Dusk*

The sun has just retired for the night amid the voices of a billion peepers on a thousand small farm ponds. Spring has returned on this last day of winter. I feel it as well as hear it in the sleighbell voices of the frogs.

It may not have been too cold for the mating ritual of the American woodcock, but it was certainly too cold to go looking for them. Now that a tenuous, chill spring has returned, we hope we are not too late. We come to an open field at the edge of a brushy woods to find out, and if we hear nothing at all, it is still a perfect night to be out.

The coral orange sunset is repeated in the lake. The long watercolor reflections in the water restate the almost black of the lakeside trees. A fish rises in that reflected blackness, scribing silver rings touched with orange light, as if for the pure pleasure of it.

We hear a barking in the distance. As the sound comes nearer it transmogrifies into the staccato honking of a pair of Canada geese. They are coming in for the night to safe harbor on open water. Moments later the rest of the resident flock follow as if on a slack rope, their voices loud across the water. They could be in our laps for the sound of it. They are black origami shapes against that reflected jack-'o-lantern sky, so low to the water their wing tips dimple its surface as they fold slowly up and down. At last the birds brake, pull up short, and kick up ruffles of silver with their big webbed feet. As they settle in, they change their tune; their high-flying honks become lower, more intimate, as if they are saying their sleepy good nights to one another.

We met a friend on the path—Wendy McDougal—who told us she had seen a pair of woodcocks by this one small meadow only moments before. But as we stand now in the growing dark at the edge of the clearing we hear only their distant practice scales, ascending and descending on a different meadow somewhere over the wooded hill.

It is the sound of a male cock's wings as he performs his aerial mating ritual, a chippering, songlike sound that changes to a warble as he plummets earthward and the wind whistles through his feathers. Now, we hear only a single, nasal, metallic *beezt*—the woodcock's true song—as we walk in silence toward the meadow.

At last we see this football-shaped bird. We disturbed his dance, and he skates off along the shoreline looking for privacy. We can see that distinctive darning-needle bill as he flies past open water as if he darned up the ragged, late-winter weeds. His short wings, making a sweet trilling sound, trail a kind of song behind him.

There is only a wisp of moon, the barest shaving, to mark our way back. But the shadow form of the moon's round body is clearly discernible above the crescent as it nears moonset. The bright-lit paring of new moon is like a fine porcelain bowl filled to overflowing with yeasty, dark dough that threatens to spill over in the growing warmth.

MARCH 21 • *Dusk*

Tonight we see no sign of woodcocks, hear no trilling. But the night is not a loss by any means. We drove to a different spot to try our luck and catch two magnificent white-tailed deer in our headlights' beams. Quickly we park and douse the lights, and the deer go only a few anxious yards before accepting our presence—warily. They look back over their shoulders at us as if daring us to follow, or inviting us. I do not know. Their ambiguity is alien, and I wish I could interpret their unspoken signals. I feel right, comfortable with them on this darkening meadow, as if we had met here by mutual agreement. At last they wander down between the overgrown meadow and a small, singing pond.

Peepers racket their sweet, piercing songs into the dusk, so loud it is almost unbearable. Almost, but not quite. I am impaled by sound, held helpless here by its wild Celtic piping as if by atavistic spell. It means spring to me—more than the bobbing dash of robins in my grass, more than the first dooryard crocus, more than the tender thready stems of rue anemone in the woods. It is hard to break that spell, woven dense with sound waves from before recorded time.

But I drag myself away to try the lake path again, looking for the woodcock's display. He proves elusive. I feel like an intruder, a wan supplicant. This display was not meant for my eyes, and he seems determined that I will not observe the ritual. I feel like a medieval would-be apprentice trying to catch the wizard in his act, trying to convince him to take me on. I am bold enough to try this sneaky, lightfoot intrusion—I only want to watch.

As we near the meadow we see a silvery wake down the long arm of a tiny feeder creek that leads to the lake. We stop to discover what draws this moving *vee* in the water. At first I take the swimmer for a muskrat, but my binoculars say different. A big beaver pulls himself out on the bank, his flat tail steadies him. I cannot tell what he is after; whatever it is, he does not find it. As if in a silent movie, he drops back into the water and continues toward us. We hold our breath; will he swim directly under our toes on the little bridge? He will not. He disappears into blackness at a sharp turn in the creek.

The little meadow just ahead is far from silent: robins still give voice at 7:00 P.M., quick, descending notes that seem to scold us for intruding—*tut-tut-tut*. We hear the geese, invisible in the shadows of the far shore. Sleepy passerines sign off for the night at the edges of the woods. We wait in unbroken silence, but the woodcocks do not appear. Only a bobbing will-'o-the-wisp of white marks an Eastern cottontail's progress through the underbrush.

MARCH 23 • *Night*

The excited baritone baying of the coonhound tangled with the thread of my dream and jerked me backward from the present tense to the past, then catapulted me into reality when the thread stretched too far. Now I wake with a groggy start, trying to make sense of what I hear just outside my window.

It is the coonhound, close and freed somehow from his fenced yard and from my dream. He is yelping at something just outside, and he warbles that he has it cornered.

I hotfoot it out the back door into spring. The air is soft and warm, and if my bare feet were used to their unprotected condition, this excursion would be pure pleasure—if still staggering and sleepy. I cannot move fast enough; each footstep is painful as I gingerly pick my way over wood chips and pebbles. But I can hear the coon scrabbling up a slippery elm at the edge of my garden, just above the wooden fence. I see his lighter shape against the darkness and catch him in midascent with my light.

For a moment the dog goes wild, yodels like a maniac, and then runs off in a panic. I did not even have the chance to yell at him to be quiet. Strange antics for a dog bred to tree his prey and stay there, come what may.

I catch the raccoon in my flashlight beam. Its eyes flash green at me like Scarlett O'Hara, then he, too, is gone, rapelling backwards, then forwards down the tree and making off across the back fence. I can hear his rustling progress through the abandoned garden and up the wooded hill.

It is all odd, off kilter, this fast-forward dream of a coon hunt played out in my backyard in the middle of the night. I would swear I was still dreaming but for each uncomfortable barefoot step over a winter's accumulation of debris.

The action is over, and bed sounds great. I give up the chase with a last luxurious sigh for the wonderful weather, the rare, sudden silence so deep I could scoop it up with a bucket.

MARCH 24 • *Night*

There is a soft whispering under the dead leaves that still lie thick on the ground in the protected places. The air smells of rain, but that is not the sound I hear. There is only a kind of airborne damp and no real rainfall.

I stand silently, barely breathing, to listen to the off-again, on-again sibilance, trying to pinpoint the sound. Here. No, there. And here again. Under the leaves, there; I saw one move. Earthworms, or emergent insects; what else could it be? It is as if the earth itself is waking from its long silence, rising from its seasonal hibernation.

Curiosity is a powerful substance manufactured in the brain. "What's *that?*" is no casual question. It demands an answer. Musings are not enough. I go for my flashlight.

I sit poised like a hunting fox to catch the faintest rustle. This miniature sound wave I wait for must be at the lowest reaches of human hearing—lost in the blowy dark—perhaps as low as forty to fifty hertz out of a possible auditory response range of twenty to approximately ten thousand hertz. My auditory nerve is finely tuned and commanded to hear. All the nerve fibers are on alert. I feel like a spy.

Each time I hear that tiny rustling I pounce and dig through the leaves to dry soil. Each time there is nothing, or nothing I can see, at any rate, nothing that could make that sound. Once, I find a miniscule white mite on a pilgrimage over the hard, inhospitable earth, but he is too small to initiate any sound at all, at least one I am capable of hearing.

But at last I discover my noisemakers. A bright band

of box-elder bugs erupts from a crack in the dry earth, crawling over one another like clowns pouring from an impossibly tiny car. In my flashlight beam their black bodies, scribed with red, look festive, as if a spring carnival had come to town just beneath the last of winter's leaves.

MARCH 25 • *Early evening*

March winds have suddenly gone berserk. A spring storm has turned to momentary terror. I feel like a cowering child looking out into nothingness in the sudden dark. Cooling temperatures bully the resident warmth, bumping hard. There is sound and fury enough even for Shakespeare in the Missouri sky.

The spring thunderstorm turns ugly; wind blows flat out across the earth, so hard I cannot see anything from the windows in my house. In my studio, water shoots in torrents between the double-glassed window and its frame. We try to see from the door, but the neighborhood has been swallowed by a blown opaqueness. We cannot hear each other shout across the space of a single room.

And as quickly as it blew up, it is over. There is still rain and lightning, but the wind has passed—halfway to Ohio by now.

We survey the damage, stepping careful as cats over downed limbs and debris. The porch trellis was blown off, broken and scattered across the yard—a visual aid to wind direction. The wind sock could not do better.

Caught up in the roar of the wind, we did not even hear the box-elder tree go down. We did not hear it scrape against the house. Fully a third of the old tree ripped loose. The noise must have been immense, buried in the wall of sound. Only the tips of the branches brushed the outside wall. If the wind had been just that much from the south, if the tree had been five feet taller, it would have been in the living room. We can see its pale, exposed heartwood in the half light.

MARCH 26 • *Predawn*

It is still dark, but the scent of the broken tree is strong on the air, a reminder of the night's violence. But against the glowing skylight, I can see the dark forms of birds perched on the newly horizontal branches. They are assessing the damage or taking the change for granted, philosophical fatalists that they are.

I am not so accepting. The loss of a tree is depressing to me; the loss of a third of this one is a wrench. We had just bought the land, the tree was my own, as much as anyone can "own" something so large. I feel a responsibility and a kind of pain. I am determined to save as much of it as possible, though it is no beauty now. Truncated, off balance, it is still shade and life, home to the birds that have begun nesting there.

Spring is tender and beautiful, a half-spoken, half-kept covenant. Only a sentimental fool, however, can overlook its deadly fickle nature, the threat that backhands that sweet promise.

MARCH 30 • *Evening*

Chorus frogs call in the small swamp by Fishing River. Their voices are different from the spring peepers—different, but as welcome. In a few weeks I will see their miniscule young waggling like sentient drops of tar through the stagnant water of the oxbow swamp.

The little swamp—a still, life-rich lake—was left like a footprint by the last capricious channel change of the river some forty years ago. An old city map shows the river where the woods and swamp are today. Some ancient flood must have ripped the new creekbed through the earth, thrown itself against the base of the clay and limestone cliff on the south, and gone no farther. It left the little oxbow where it lay, abandoned it to its own devices.

And the little body of water was not without resources. It slowly filled with life in abundance. Not the *same* life as that of the creek, though at first it was indistinguishable: crayfish and small bass, shiners and bottom-feeding catfish. But eventually the turtles moved in, staked a claim, and now decorate each fallen log like tiles in the summer, splashing off into the silent water if I come too close. In spring the water is alive with frogs, billions of them bobbing up between granular bits of duckweed. If I did not see them, I would know they were here by the urgent voices of an early spring night. The frogs and I are grateful for the change in the old channel—they, for a welcoming habitat, and I for the chance to see them there.

MARCH 31 • *Night*

The Missouri Department of Conservation's Natural Events Calendar gives this date as the average day of last frost in Southern Missouri, and I envy my southern neighbors. We may have many more days of frost in this northwest corner of the state. Tonight frost glitters on the moonlit wintry grass. The days are warming, sweet and scented, but night is still the province of the cold.

APRIL 3 • *Early Morning*

The morning brings clarity and sun after an otherwise tempestuous week. An Alberta clipper sailed down from Canada straight across the northern Missouri border—all sheets flying—freezing fruit tree blossoms and jonquils in its wake and covering many parts of the country in an icy whiteness. The viscous fluid that is the lifeblood of my daffodils froze solid overnight. When I pick a bouquet to brighten the breakfast table, they break just at that spot where the sap crystallized like water in a drinking straw.

When afternoon comes the ones that are left will flop face down on the sidewalk like so many Bowery drunks.

The young redbud tree, which for the first time was covered with tight magenta buds, felt the chill of night. Most of the buds are blackened and limp and will not open. A few—about as many as bloomed during its first and second springs—will open as if nothing had happened. I wonder why two thirds of the buds on one branch were hit, while others, only inches away, were spared? It is the same all over the tree: two or three blackened, shrunken bud clusters, then one as bright and full of life as ever.

This is the second spring in a row that has felt the back of winter's departing hand, a rebuke for too much giddy gaiety. The orchardists nearby have stood the night watch, spraying their trees with a mist of water to coat the blossoms with ice—an odd overcoat to protect the tender blossoms from the frigid night, but the air's temperature has gone considerably below that at which water freezes. The thin ice coating protects the buds from these extremes.

The men must be careful how much they spray: too little, and it will do no good; too much, and the branches will break under the weight Still, the night's losses are not cause for despair. Like most who work on the land, the orchardists do not give up easily. At bedrock there is always optimism—for what is saved, for next year's crop—otherwise there would be no one left on the land at all.

APRIL 4 • *Predawn*

Crows are silently escorting a barred owl from tree to tree through the park. With wings extended, they are nearly as large as he is.

It is early morning, just before sunup. The owl must have been planning a long day's nap from the labors of hunting, but the crows have other ideas. They move like graceful black shadows, slipping through the trees like the night itself, mobbing the owl, forcing him to leave each perch. There are five of them, and the owl seems to feel that prudence is the wisest course—a retreat is in order.

At night the owl owns the hill. I often hear him at his hunt or conversing with a mate: *who-cooks-for-you, who-cooks-for-you-all-l-l?*

APRIL 9 • *Evening*

A squirrel is taking a late nap—or an early bed—in the tree just overhead. I have never seen one so bold, snoozing with so much fine unconcern, and without so much as a dead leaf for a lounging platform.

At first I cannot believe it is a live squirrel. Usually they are so alert and active in the daylight hours, scattering from my approach like children from the boogeyman. But this one simply lies there in a warm brown wad.

My binoculars are no help, at first; the dimming light has flattened all forms, robbing them of their three-dimensionality. The squirrel's back is to me, in any case. With the magnification of the already amazingly close animal he looks too big to be a single squirrel. His odd position only adds to the confusion, I can barely make out body parts. Are there two squirrels tangled overhead?

Finally I walk next door for a better look, and the squirrel rouses just enough to fix me with one sleepy eye. I make squirrel noises at him, and he moves his head slightly to look, but takes no further notice—I might be a leaf for all he cares.

My night glasses boost my vision, and I am able to see this fat fellow better. He has an elm seed hanging from his mouth, as if he were simply too full to eat another bite. Has he gorged himself into a drowsy torpor in my tree? Or is he ill? This is most uncharacteristic behavior for the squirrels that frequent my backyard. I hope he has not gotten into the poison put out for the rats that moved in next door after the fire.

Later, after full dark, I take my flashlight to the tree to see how he has fared. He is gone at last, perhaps to the hole in the big maple out front for a night's sleep uninterrupted by a curious naturalist. But just to make sure he has not fallen, I make one more foray next door, searching the ground as well as the slender limbs he clung to.

APRIL 11 • *Evening*

The soil of the old garden in our fenced yard is beautiful, tilled, and ready for this year's delights and disappointments and surprises. The smell of the minute soil microbes, which speaks of early spring, fills the air, accentuated by the cool night air.

It is time for toads to come out of their winter burrows. How auspicious that one has come out of hiding just as we have tilled the garden. This beneficial insect-eater is a welcome resident in my backyard.

I hold him in my hand for a while to study his markings. He turns that thick sumo wrestler's neck to look at me with distaste—how dare I not have warts and bowlegs, when the night begs for toad romance? His stance is like a Japanese wrestler's as well—those fat sides and strong thighs are powerful, pushing against my restraining hands. He jumps away from my grasp almost without effort.

I do quick sketches by lantern light from as many positions as I can, but he makes his deep dislike for the process known. He exudes a white, poisonous fluid through his skin, like sap from a milkweed stem. This liquid irritates the mouth or eyes—a toad's protection against hungry predators. I reward him for his modeling with a broken flowerpot condo on the edge of the garden. There he will be out of harm's way and convenient to the many chewing and sucking insects drawn to my defenseless produce.

He is a Fowler's toad; his markings give his identity away as surely as my pale skin and blue eyes tell of my northern European roots. This fellow is one of our most common toads, found throughout much of the country. I wonder if he is the same toad I drew out from under the storage cabinet on the back porch two years ago? He could have grown this much, and he might have stayed if the yard was a hospitable place.

Hours later, he still glowers at me with golden eyes from the depths of the shadowy pot. Perhaps he will stay if I promise not to manhandle him and keep my flashlight beam out of his eyes.

APRIL 12 • *Early*

A pair of robins visits my garden in the early morning hours. Attracted by the freshly tilled soil, they do an odd *pas de deux* over the raised beds, dipping to run a few feet so quickly I can scarcely see their legs moving. Then they stop, stand erect, stretch their necks, and, in unison, tap the earth with their tails as if to assure themselves that it is still there. They stand and listen, heads cocked, then dip and dart away again. Their ballet is joined by a jay and a sparrow. A female cardinal is attracted by the hunt. For a tiny garden, mine seems to have attracted quite a crowd of breakfasters, like the little café in town, full of farmers and other early birds.

APRIL 14 • *Midnight*

The night air intensifies odors; the interweaving scents are strong and fresh. Some, familiar and loved, catch my attention first—sweet williams bloom in the forgotten garden across the alley, my geraniums fill the air with spice. The scent of earth in my recently tilled garden is as sweet as any flower.

The cut grass, now two days gone, sends a reminder in its fresh hay smell; Harris has used the clippings as mulch on the garden. It holds down weeds and keeps the moisture in the soil, unless the nesting robins take it all. Gill-over-the-ground is spicy, as well; my nose prickles with its scent as I walk on the unseen plants hugging the ground. If I were blind instead of simply wandering in the night, I would still know when the ground ivy greens up in the spring.

Even the woodpile has a fine, midnight scent that is as comforting looming in the darkness as it is in January when lit and smokey. It is security still, even in April.

Other scents mingle, overlapping as subtly as the territories of the creatures that inhabit this corner of Missouri. There is an olfactory patchwork wrapped around my backyard.

If I were closer to the creek I would smell its sweet scent of mud and algae and life. In the woods nearby, mushrooms shoulder from the ground, building themselves from the lacy macramé of mycelium hidden beneath the leaf mold. They add their rich, fungal smells to the April night.

And on the hill the farmland scents surround our valley town.

There are the warm, animal scents of cattle and sheep and horses, the scent of hay still laid up in the barn, of tilled fields teeming with actino-mycetes.

APRIL 15 • *Predawn*

Robins fill every square inch of the predawn light with their lilting, rol-licking songs, like the psalmist's joy that "cometh in the morning." I hear a singing male announcing his satisfaction with territory and mate and life in general. On the hill another sings in counterpoint and, up the street, another adds his trill. If I listen carefully I can sort out the concert; each neighborhood has its singer from here to as far distant as I can hear. It blends into a constant, seamlessly blanketing my corner of the world, and, thanks to Rachel Carson and her milestone book, *Silent Spring*, dawn birdsong reaches from California to New York with only slight variations in individual singers.

Here in my own backyard the song is hardly exclusively robin. A cardinal high in an oak repeats his *pretty, pretty, pretty*—and so it is. The *peter-peter* of titmice and the sweet two-note of chickadees join in as the light becomes stronger. A crow passes overhead, his loud and atonal cry, like cymbals, punctuating his straightforward flight. Over by the river I can hear two more, cawing conversationally as they fly.

Jays have been awakened and add their musical *tool-ools* to the song. If it were anything but nature's own moving music, I would complain of cacophony.

Is everyone intent on claiming or reclaiming territory from the night? Is that what all this loud, morning proclamation is all about? I am quite content to have "my" territory—bought with arbitrary paper funds of questionable and fluctuating value—claimed by these more rightful and more ancient of owners.

APRIL 17 • *Midnight*

On the hill a dog breaks the silence with his sudden baying. His voice splits the night and is answered by another and another, until all the dogs on this side of town have joined in the instinctive howling. The neighborhood "wolf pack" is loud in defending its territory, and an inter-loper has invaded. I see his pale form moving toward me through the deserted garden. He lumbers on, unseeing, makes his way closer with a

whisper of sound, ignoring me as if I were not there. It is the opossum that winters in my basement coming home after an early evening foray. Even in the dark his black-tipped, silvery fur gives his identity away from halfway across the yard, that and his rolling sailor's gait. I hear the clunk and bang of the water pipes that half block his entrance hole in our stone foundation. He has embroidered his Home Sweet Home over the hole with bits of fur and oak leaves tugged after him for a den.

One by one the dogs fall silent—danger avoided, interloper routed, territory defended.

I would have thought the nocturnal opossum would go out to hunt at night—or that he was gone for the summer—but instead I hear him rattling among the cat food cans. He has come home for dinner.

The rattles escalate, and there is a wild hissing, audible even from outside the house. He must have had another territorial dispute, this time with the resident basement cat.

After peace reigns on the landing, I fetch the flashlight to see if the visitor has eaten—though I am sure from the loud, rapid chewing heard through the door that he is making short work of the cat food. He is there, small eyed and trusting, looking up at me. His dinner is hard won; a bleeding gouge is cut deep into his forehead, a souvenir of my rough old tomcat.

APRIL 18 • *Predawn*

They say the dawn wind rises with the sun, pushing away the last of the night. But try as I might I have never caught the moment of its coming. The trees are still, still as a held breath, waiting. Nothing moves on the hill. Not a leaf stirs in the redbud tree over my head. These big sail-like leaves will catch the slightest breeze, dancing madly, wearing their hearts on their sleeves, but they are still as death as I wait for that apocryphal wind.

Will the dawn wind push this still night air ahead of it in a scented, billowing, birdsong ripple, like a bedsheet shaken to smooth out its wrinkles? Sunrise comes late to my backyard, tucked snug against the east hill. The swifts overhead are lit already, tinted pink as Easter eggs. The sky is pastel, pale blue now, and the eastern pink has bleached to a golden salmon. It will be a half hour and more before dawn touches its moving fingers to my face as I sit with my eyes to the mecca of the sunrise, expecting dawn wind.

I rise stiffly to look behind me; sunrise has come already to the western hills. They are lit up, painted golden and buttery with a wide, soft brush. If the dawn wind billowed the air, it skipped over my head like a stone on the rippled surface of a lake. The trees there are active as breakers on the shore, the wind has come with the sun, and I missed it again. Coffee and the morning paper and my cozy chair sound good to me now.

APRIL 19 • *Sundown*

Full dark drags its heels. Sundown extinguishes only the round globe of the sun itself but not the peach pink afterglow of the sky—the light giver. This light lingers like a memory for over an hour.

I watch as the box-elder tree moves and dances with sparrows displaying, singing, chasing one another from branch to branch. One small male seems to be interested in a whole flock of puzzled females. He flutters his downturned wings at them, tail held high, hopping from first one female to another with no apparent success. Then, as the growing dark steals the light from the sky, one by one the birds disappear, winking out like morning stars.

The singer sits by the campfire, weaving our Missouri history for us with his songs; my ears are full of Jesse James, but my eyes search the slender limbs for the last of the sparrows silhouetted against the fading light. There is only one left, the male, still displaying to no one in particular. Will he simply give it up, stop and sleep, head under wing? Will he disappear into the hole I see in the trunk to a snug night nest? But somehow between one note and the next I lose sight of him. The growing dusk renders the world flat and one dimensional as a child's drawing—the sparrow I believe I am watching is nothing more than a leaf blown gently in the wind.

APRIL 21 • *Morning*

Watching the early morning feeding antics of a small band of English sparrows on my lawn, I wonder if this is a specialized dawn-feeding trick to capture sleepy insects too cold and stiff to fly? My four sparrows are hovering like hummingbirds, a foot or two off the ground, wings beating madly. They move a few feet to a new patch of green, then hover again, staring intently downward. They look a bit like novice helicopter pilots just learning the rudiments of landing and takeoff, and, in fact, I would think they were juveniles in practice if they were not wearing adult plumage and intent on insects in the grass.

Every so often, one of the birds will float to the ground and snatch at a bit of breakfast. I can see wings and long legs protruding from the small beaks. And one little bird cannot decide whether to build a home or catch her breakfast. Her beak is stuffed with bits of grass, but she still hovers above the feeding ground with the rest. There is hardly room for grass and bug in that tiny mouth, and her luck in catching insects is abysmal.

APRIL 22 • *Night*

We took a bedtime walk around the neighborhood to sample the night. Spring is the time for fast-moving change after a winter of changes visible only in time-lapse sequence. We wanted to see what might be about.

The nighthawks that hunt the airways just over town have returned from wintering in South America; their loud, buzzy *crank* or *peent* startles us, a sudden bombardment of sound from the otherwise silent sky. It is a sound I associate with warm summer nights, and pleasantly. Its jarring harshness bothers me not at all.

This jay-sized bird is misnamed. Neither hawk nor strictly nocturnal, the nighthawk is often heard around here in broad daylight—it is a versatile hunter.

Nighthawks are members of the same family as whippoorwills (Caprimulgae), but their calls are far more infrequent. Last year at this time, according to my field journal, we were already hearing the nighthawk's sweetly repetitious cousin in the woods near the river.

APRIL 23 • *Night*

The nights are almost devoid of insect noises, so unlike the din of full summer. The cycle is only just now beginning; a series of warm nights will bring more and more singers.

Tonight we heard the first soloist practicing her scales in anticipation of the concert—a cricket's voice, all alone and not a part of the *a cappella* chorus, sounds oddly sad.

If this is a field cricket warming up, she overwintered as an egg implanted deep in my neighbor's soil. Tree cricket eggs are sealed into thick, corky bark of tree limbs with the excrement secreted by the female. They stay snug until spring in this insulating blanket. These nymphs usually mature in midsummer. Our midnight singer is getting a jump on things.

It is impossible to tell from that lonely song which kind of cricket we are listening to; my ear is out of practice from last year's insect opera. I would have to see the singer to identify it and, since the sound emanated from the bushes near a darkened house, I would rather not be taken for a prowler just to see a bug.

APRIL 25 • *Night*

The night song is intensified by darkness. Sounds are loud in the sonar of my mind. I can hear a truck out on the highway beyond the town, shifting down for the long, slow descent.

Someone is up in a light plane playing with the dark. The engine hums like an oversized mosquito; the plane seems to be trying out maneuvers. I hear the hum change and deepen and change again.

The first of the June bugs has put in an early appearance. He plays percussion on the window screens of my studio. Where I sit in the darkness half a backyard away, I hear the buzz of sound under his hard, glossy carapace, then the staccato *bang bang* as he hits the aluminum screen, making for the light. The kittens play counterpoint rhythm to his drumbeat. Each time he bangs the screen Meeskeit pounces back at him with a soft, fur-cushioned impact, and Zola swats at him in rapid-fire volleys.

APRIL 26 • *Early*

The sodden garden after the midnight thunderstorm is alive with mating pairs of pink, fleshy earthworms, stretched full-length from their burrow holes, one end on home base. They are held firmly in place by hairlike *cetae*. They are hermaphroditic; each bears male and female reproductive organs, but they still must fertilize each other's eggs with sperm to assure a future supply of healthy wigglers to populate my garden. During mating they glue themselves together with a sticky solution excreted at the swollen ring — the saddle or clitellum — each bears at the front of its body.

The worms are unmolested by the robins, sparrows, and jays that usually feed in the quiet morning hours. Are the bigger birds put off by the loud, territorial claims of the wrens that woke me from sleep? One perches high on the television antenna over the house, still claiming all he can see for his own. The male cardinal that normally claims that aluminum high ground has been displaced by a bird half his size.

By the time the sun breaks over the hill and sends the first long fingers of light snaking through the backyard, the worms have all returned to their burrows, safe for another day.

APRIL 27 • *Evening*

The backyard is suddenly as full of raucous voices as the 1968 Democratic convention. Jays are loud in their disapproval—of something—and I turn off the stove burner and go to investigate. The young elm at the corner of the yard is alive with jays, cardinals, robins, and the wren that is taking up residence in the next tree. Could they be mobbing an owl?

The leaves have grown so quickly that I cannot see what might be hidden there until I get closer to the trunk itself. About halfway up, a nearly full-grown black snake, glossy as black leather, is wrapped around a fork in the tree. His small, bullet head is bobbing up and down hypnotically, somehow managing to take in all of his attackers at once.

I race to the house for my sketchbook; it is too good an opportunity to miss, and the snake is immobilized by the ruckus. The wren's nest is safe enough—for now.

I get as close as I can despite a more or less constant barrage from Harris: "Be careful. Don't let it bite you. Don't get too close. Don't let it fall on you. Don't touch it. Stay *back*." Men have been chary of snakes ever since the Garden; my husband is no exception, though his distaste is tempered with fascination.

I shoo him back into the house so I can sketch in peace. Either my presence so close to the black snake has calmed the mobbing flock of songbirds, or it has driven them away. Now it is only me, the snake, and the pugnacious little wren.

I am astounded. Time after time this tiny four-and-a-half-inch bird advances on the four-foot snake, feints, jabs, feints again like a featherweight boxer in the ring with a heavyweight. He is totally silent—none

of the chattering, scolding stutters he normally reserves for me or for the cats. This time he is focused like a laser, deadly concentrated on vanquishing the threat from his territory and, more importantly, from the wren house less than six feet away in the next tree.

The wren attacks from all angles, hopping down the trunk headfirst like a nuthatch, flying to the nearest twig, and finally hopping to within an inch of the snake's snub-nosed snout. It is a tiny, feathered David in combat with a Goliath, and the little bird is determined to prevail.

If I were an entirely dispassionate observer, I would simply stand and watch to see the end of the stalemate. The snake's mouth does not look large enough to swallow the wren whole, but I know that it is. Those jaws disjoint to a disconcerting cavern. They go after eggs, small rodents, and baby birds, mostly. But his fat, sleek sides most definitely *do* look big enough to contain his tiny adversary.

I cannot wait around to see. Harris comes to the door to check on me, and I ask him to bring me the garden hoe. Working carefully so as not to harm the snake, I untwine him gently from the trunk. He makes as if to escape and slither out of my reach into the leaf canopy, but I cut him off at the pass and wrap him instead around the hoe. I can feel his serpentine embrace. With a flip of the hoe I toss him into the abandoned garden across the alley. He sails end for end and lands in a thick cushion of weeds. I poke among them with my hoe, encouraging him to retreat, threatening mayhem if he does not. The movement in the tall weeds tells me he is headed away from the elm. I slump in relief, confrontation avoided.

The eerily silent wren explodes into song, filling the late-evening air until the backyard reverberates with sound. I imagine a note of triumph in his territorial anthem.

Harris hopes the wren family will abandon their homestead and raise babies elsewhere. He is sure the snake will return to eat the eggs. I do not give it that much credit for intelligence or memory. I feel like the victor in our little drama.

But my victory celebration is premature; I am wrong. It seems my husband was the wiser: his scenario was correct. A short time later, I see the snake has returned to his deadly errand, and he is up the right tree this time. The wren house is only inches away. My interventions on the wren family's behalf have only worsened their danger.

I try to pull him off again and fail. I try again and succeed, but the snake drops off my hoe before I can deposit him harmlessly into the picnic cooler for a trip to the park. He escapes into the interstices of the woodpile.

It is cat and mouse now. How long will he hide there? The cooling night must make him inactive. And what will I do if I catch him again on his way up the tree? Kill him? I do not want to, but the wrens are welcome residents—avatars of memory and joy—and the snake has proven himself both smart and cunning, if beneficial to my garden.

The rat snake has no fear of me, nor I of him, and we are both deadly intent on that wren house. It may be a long wait. I have all the time in the world, at least until it gets too dark to see a black snake in the night.

APRIL 28 • *Early*

A bumblebee has roused before the competition to forage in my garden. His thick furry overcoat allows him to move about much earlier than the other pollinators. I watch as he clings upside down to the comfrey flowers, probing each in turn with that glistening proboscis, like a kid at a soda fountain. His fat abdomen bobs rhythmically, as if he rocks himself with contentment.

APRIL 30 • *Nightfall*

We play at hide and seek with the owls at the edge of the woods. We brought our tape deck, complete with owl call tapes, just to see if we might initiate a conversation with the park's resident nocturnal hunters. I like to know my neighbors.

I have heard them before in the night woods, and I have seen them resting in the deep shade during the day, hiding their easily dazzled eyes from the light. These are barred owls. Their kitten faces turn curiously toward me when I visit the woods, their deep brown eyes bottomless as the night sky.

We came just before full dark. The woods are flat and gray like cardboard sets from a stage play, but the sky is still filled with peach and aqua light. Whatever we find tonight will stand out easily against that brilliance.

We discovered the perfect observatory: a narrow peninsula of open grassland bounded on three sides with thick, old-growth forest—part of the new Missouri Natural Area. Here we can tuck ourselves invisibly into the edge of the woods and still have a clear view of a strip of sky unobstructed by branches and leaves.

At first, when we crank up the tape—the great horned owl, the screech owl, the barred owls most common in this corner of Missouri—the only respondents are sleepy songbirds, disturbed in their bedtime rituals. They soon quiet down, though, and return to their roosts. Do they recognize the electronic nature of our owls?

When the screech owl's small, quavering voice fills the woods with its eerie wails, it is instantly answered by a repeated hissing from a near-by tree. Is there a baby screecher there calling for an imagined parent? Or perhaps the more uncommon barn owl, seldom seen in this part of Missouri? We can find nothing in the deep, still shadows.

I am anticipating the effect of the barred owl's canned calls—deep and booming. It always gets the best response, even from daylight song-birds who mob my tape player. And I am not disappointed. At the first recorded call, an answer comes from up on the hill. Immediately, from somewhere behind us, another owl calls, answering the first—its mate. They have mistaken our tape for each other, or else they confer about the whereabouts of the intruder, triangulating our position audibly with those big efficient ears hidden on each side of the facial disc.

You don't see an owl's true ears, not even on the long-eared or short-eared owls. Those are simply feather tufts. (A great-horned owl has no horns, either—the odd configuration of feathers just makes it appear that way.)

An owl's true ears are tucked behind the soft feathers of a somewhat dish-shaped face. The facial shape, and the facial feathers as well, funnel sound to the ears, which are offset to collect sound waves from slightly different quadrants. As the nocturnal bird swivels his head, cocks it to one side, or moves it from side to side, he hears everything there is to hear. It is a most efficient set-up; he could catch prey in full dark.

As soon as they have a fix on us—and each other—they fall deadly silent. We wait, calling into the gathering dusk, wondering if the game is up. But no. A silent shape flies between us and the bright half-moon, keeping behind the screen of leaves. We see its movement more than its shape, and we point, excitedly, like children.

It is joined by another owl shape, this one just overhead in the clear-ing. It swoops low, swivelling that big head for a better look. The short, broad wings, perfectly engineered for flying missions among the trees, are easily visible—primaries extended like reaching fingers, each feather spotted with brown.

We continue our one-sided conversation with the owls—playing and replaying the recorded calls—and are rewarded with their repeated reconnaissance missions above our heads. Their flight is chillingly and unbelievably silent for such big birds. Their wing feathers are fringed with soft borders to filter the air to silence. If it had been full dark we never would have seen them, never would have known that the owl pair was sizing us up, over and over, silently patrolling the air above our heads. If we were mice we would be in deep trouble.

EARLY SUMMER

The Mellow Months

THE VOLATILE DAYS OF EARLY SPRING ARE GONE, the days when we could not hazard a guess as to what would happen next: what the weather would be, which wildflower would bloom in an unexpected place, what memory would be stirred by ephemeral scents on the night air. It is early summer, and we begin to feel as if we know what we are about. The worst threat of tornadic activity has passed, though that catastrophic weather pattern is still a possibility. We begin to breathe easier. The exquisite uncertainty, which rubs nerves raw while it stirs something strange in the blood, is being replaced, day by day, with a knowing, with an acceptance, a peace. It is sometimes shattered.

The smell of freshly cut grass is on the night air, so pure and strong we swear we can see it as well as smell it. In the country, the scent of newly mown hay lies languid across the darkened meadows.

Night-blooming flowers trail pale delicate fingers through the air, sending olfactory messages to nocturnal insect pollinators. Evening primrose, nightshade, marsh marigold, night-flowering catchfly, butterfly orchis, even the imported Japanese honeysuckle are pollinated by night. They combine a dark-hour scent—lush and intense—with distinctive design and light colors to attract their night-specific benefactors. By way of thanks, these insects carry pollen from flower to flower, assuring continuity.

Bats and other small mammals share in the work of pollinating as they go about their nocturnal business. Moles, voles, and mice are active looking for mates and defining territory or satisfying the needs of early spring litters. Shrews continue their endless metabolic quest for more food and still more food to fill bellies that are never satiated. All carry the dust of pollen as they go.

A female mosquito seeks the protein of fresh blood to form her eggs; only the female plays this vampire role and most insistently at dusk and dawn. Every stagnant pool squirms with her thrashing, shrimplike young.

As early summer progresses, we hear the metallic songs of cicadas in the late afternoon and evening. They have dug their way out of the earth, still wearing their larval armor. They shed it to find their wings and voices, stridulating madly in the growing dark. The long streamers of eggs, left by frogs and toads in chilly spring ponds, have hatched. Now the young are developing legs and taking to the land like our earliest ancestors—oddly human with their muscled Olympic thighs. After the spring rush, we hear the adults much less frequently; they sing in ones and twos, if at all. The exuberant mating choir of spring has dispersed. One by one the small frogs skulk silent through the woods or send their piercing notes out over a creek.

The first of summer's fruits ripen in the night—strawberries and mulberries. Elderflowers glow like incandescent seafoam in the darkness. They, too, are good to eat. We make a fine tea of them to serve with elder blow fritters on the deck at night.

Whippoorwills repeat their plaintive song deep into these hours to find a mate and—who knows?—perhaps for the sheer orneriness of it. The calls go on for hours, sanding away at our patience.

The blue, atmospheric haze of late summer has not yet formed. The pounding heat that stifles the long nights of July and August has barely hinted at its advent, and earth is not yet hammerlocked in its grip. It is clear and lovely and early summer, whatever the calendar may say.

MAY 3 • *Early*

First light is gray and watery after the hard rain. The new seeds in the garden will have done well to stay in their shallow furrows; there was almost two inches of rain contained in those downpours.

The house wren is awake and loud in his greeting of such a gray day. He patrols newly won territory, scolding and singing his exuberant, bubbling song. His mate has joined him, and together they stitch diagonals back and forth across the yard, sewing it up neatly and labelling it their own.

MAY 4 • *2:00 A.M.*

My thunder-fearing cat has alerted me to the coming storm. When we went to bed last night the clouds had barely made their inroads in the sky. A rumble or two passed overhead without incident, and I thought the predicted storm was just another promise to be broken.

But at 2:00 A.M., Reuben jumped crying to my hip, waking me. I could barely hear the faint grumbling in the sky; it sounded like distant cannons in a dream of war. He would not be put off. Cat ears as well as cat eyes must be more finely tuned than mine, and he was right. The artillery barrage breasted the far edge of the bowl of hills and snagged itself in our hollow. Cloud cannons ricocheted around and around the valley for fully an hour.

The wind was at first only a rumor among the new leaves, but soon it rose to a constant howl, eerily human in timbre—chilling. The lightning strobed, and the framed angels on my bedroom walls flashed again and again like the confrontation between heaven and hell itself. It is the first real thunderstorm of this dry spring—off schedule by a month—and it seems to want to make sure we notice, no matter what time of night it sends its drum rolls through the hills.

I went outside to watch the storm for sheer pleasure. The "battle" is one in truth—the warm and cold fronts that played tug-of-war over our heads all day decided to duke it out, and the conflict is too exciting to miss. A huge electrical octopus reaches from one horizon to the other, armed with 100 million volts. This one is only sabre rattling. Nothing explodes in flames.

It is a rousing good storm, more stirring in the contrasting dark —although, at its height, there is little enough of that. Lightning is a constant. I do not need my flashlight to find my way back to bed.

MAY 5 • *Early*

I missed the phantom macramé artist again, though I am up before dawn. Yesterday a bird had found the yarn we use to mark the garden rows and had tied the redbud tree and the bird feeder pole to the old table on the patio in an attempt to steal nesting material. It is a long piece of yarn, the remains of a skein stuck into the garden cabinet on the back porch. I am amazed it was found behind the nearly closed door in the first place. Bemused, I imagine the scene as the determined nester trailed the thirty-foot length of yarn behind him. I can see his zigzag path as though he had worn a tracer.

I rolled the yarn back up and stashed it under the barbecue grill. And this morning on dawn patrol I find that the stubborn builder had rediscovered this marvelous resource and again has mimicked an oversized spider in the backyard. Yarn is everywhere, looped and tangled and woven in a very messy, very big web, indeed.

I can take a hint. Today I will capitulate, cut the yarn into short lengths and put it back out for the nest builder. It must be a robin working on his second nest of the season. Early spring's young are already spot-breasted adolescents, just smaller than their harried parents and discovering their own brand of bravado.

But before I can carry out my plan, I find to my amazement that the robin retraced his steps, untangled his web, and made off with his prize. All of it. Some fine nest will have a soft, white lining. Edwin Way Teale often remarked on these spring nesters' fondness for a bit of white. *This* nest will be as elegant as a Manhattan apartment, pale and cushioned with virgin wool.

MAY 7 • *Night*

The tiny eight-inch owlet blinked at me as if in disbelief. How had he come to be in a cage in my workroom instead of safe in his home tree

with his doting parents dancing attendance? The fleshy rims of his eyes were red and swollen, as if he had been crying. I shook my head at my own anthropomorphism.

He had taken his first flight from the nest and landed in an inopportune place—the ninth hole of the local golf course. Fledgling screech owls can only fly down, not up, for the first week or two at any rate.

He found his way to me via attentive golfers and friends with equal affection for nature's creatures. I took him to the veterinarian to check the red eyes. The vet applied ointment to soothe them but gave the owlet a clean bill of health. He spent the day in my workroom, a quiet bed and breakfast complete with bits of fresh mouse, which he ate with a perplexed gusto.

Now, just after dark, we are back at the edge of the golf course. We came prepared to return him to his anxious parents.

There is no moon, only the pinpricks of the stars and the first greenish lanterns of fireflies that punctuate the darkness. We make the only .

noises as our feet crunch over the gravel road. We brought the little gray-phase bird in his borrowed cage and a tape deck with screech owl calls. We hope to call in the parent birds and stage a reunion.

It works. We put the owlet in a bush beside the road, step back and crank up the tape. It seems only seconds before we hear the little owl's childish quaver in response to the tape. We wait in the deeper shadows by the road. The parent owls recognize their own and swoop in, furtive as guerrillas against the sky. We see movement and the suggestion of broad, stubby wings. We hear the whistling call—real owl, this time, not taped. The baby answers. We see his light shape fly toward them in short swoops through the low brush, and theirs come to meet him. We are as relieved as we imagine them to be and let out our collective breach in a *whoosh*. We had been trying not to breathe, unwittingly, trying not to make a sound, trying to blend into the dark, hoping for homecoming.

MAY 9 • *Evening*

An early evening ride in the country reveals many diurnal creatures that have not yet retired and night-active animals that are just coming out to feed. It is the changing of the guard.

We startle a female killdeer at her nest on a back-country cul-de-sac. At first I do not realize what we are seeing, only that she is uncharacteristically unafraid of our car as we circle her, turning around to go back the way we had come.

She stands her ground, bobbing slightly on those thin, sticklike legs, then squats in place, nearly touching the slight hollow in the gravel. Of course! The hollow is her scrape, lined with a few pale wisps of grass. Looking closely, I can see the rounded, speckled form of a buff-colored egg beneath her. She must have just begun her brood; killdeers usually lay from three to five of these well-camouflaged eggs in their invisible nests.

She does not go into the tilting, side-angling display punctuated with piteous cries of *killdeer, killdeer* meant to lure us away. Instead, she leaves this location and pretends to incubate nearby. Then as if changing her mind or unwilling to leave her single egg, she returns and stands stubbornly firm, hovering over the scrape—unusual behavior, in my experience, anyway.

It is a good thing for the killdeer's nest that the small country housing development did not take. Both dead-end roads are just that, very dead. There is little enough traffic on the cul-de-sac. But killdeers often choose odd places for nest building: rooftops of busy shopping centers, parking lots, playing fields. They must resemble ancestral nesting grounds.

MAY 10 • *Evening*

The concrete of the old bridge—an efficient thermal sink—is warm against my forearms. The sun has slipped beneath the horizon.

Fish feed hungrily in the big pool. Mayflies have hatched, and the fish waste no time at the harvest.

A pair of kingbirds is out late, looping together over the water as if yoked. Bank swallows dive-bomb us on their way back to their tunneled holes in the clay bank upstream. They stop just short of Kamikaze. These smallest of swallows are singing, or chittering, louder than I have ever heard them, or perhaps it only seems so in the evening quiet. They have hunted together all day and now return to their nests in tandem as well.

Frogs and toads tune up down by the creek. We stand and listen to them at the edge of the woods. One trills a single, repeated note, another a kind of sustained, cricketlike song. The loud chorusing of spring peepers has ceased; it was all too short. Long enough, I suppose, for the purposes of frogs.

The birds silence themselves for the night. A crow breaks this quiet with a disgruntled cawing. We see his big black form against the still-light sky; he is on his way to join the others at roost.

The crows seem to be concentrated in a single tree down by the bend at the riffle. One by one they break cover, cawing as if to announce their intentions, and leave their perches for the deeper woods on the hill. No, they have gone, instead, to fetch the rest of the flock. A silent band of twenty to twenty-five birds breaks now from the woods and heads for the sycamores on the far side of Fishing River to roost—apparently for the night. The renegade crows do not seem to be following crow protocol. Normally, in the spring, crows travel in small bands made up of a breeding pair and their last-season offspring. They are silent but small groups. This large roosting band seems a throwback to winter's more communal habits.

MAY 11 · *Evening*

The children down the block have brought me a baby chickadee that fell from a nest. I am on my way to a meeting and am torn by the childish desire to take the little bird and try to raise it or to give this little band of wide-eyed supplicants the right answer: return it to a high place as near as possible to where you found it. Its parents will feed and care for it there.

It was so tiny, peering out between the cupped, protective palms of the oldest child. I have held an adult chickadee during bird bandings, and they are as tiny a piece of sentient, beating life as you can imagine. I ache for the touch of this one, even smaller.

But the naturalist prevails, and I give the children the correct answer, hard though it is. *Damn* a childhood that allowed me the now-forbidden pleasures of attempting to raise small robins, owlets, squirrels, rabbits, crows, whatever my father brought home from the woods. Old habits die hard. To protect wildlife from ourselves, we have passed needed legislation to prohibit keeping a wild bird or animal in private hands, and that is good. Too many small creatures were imagined to be abandoned when their parents were, in fact, watching from nearby cover to keep from drawing attention to the nest. But a life in contact with these small wild creatures did fulfill its promise. It was not *all* bad, that innocent, ignorant nurturing. I care, still. I spend my life, as much as possible, in contact with the wild, doing what I can to preserve it. (And on occasion—as with the screech owl—I still find myself in the position of temporary nanny. The opportunity affords as much pleasure as it did when I was six.)

Today's children do not have the chance for intimate communication, the chance to learn, first hand, the needs and requirements of wild things. I am sorry for their loss while I recognize the wisdom of the law.

I wonder where the chickadee baby is now. I hope nightfall found it in a safe place. If it escaped the deadly ministrations of a dozen sweaty little hands, it may escape the neighborhood cats as well.

I do not hold out too much hope for it. Last summer these same earnest children found a box turtle. They kept it and handled it until it had been dropped often enough—and hard enough—to break its shell with a great ugly gaping wound. Life is so fragile, even when it seems tough as turtle shell.

We are mutually dangerous, I suppose, nature and humankind. The turtle might have had his revenge; they carry salmonella. Illness or perhaps even death could result if hands are not washed thoroughly after handling. That is why you can no longer buy baby turtles at the pet store.

MAY 12 • *Evening*

I am startled by a loud booming just overhead, startled until I recognize that lovely summer sound for what it is—a common nighthawk booming for a mate. He makes that loud, hollow boom with his wings, not his voice box, as I once imagined. Like the American woodcock, he is making a power dive, opening his wings at the last minute as he swerves upward. The sound travels like a sonic boom. It must be an effective mating ploy. Who could miss it?

MAY 13 • *Early*

A turkey vulture is oddly out of place this early morning. He looks most incongruous as he sweeps the air with deep, repeated wingbeats—he is flying low. The sun is not yet fully up. It is too cold for the rising thermals of warmer air that the vulture usually relies on for lift under those big black windsails. I wonder where he is bound so early in the morning. Intent on his destination, he is forced to imitate the flapping flight of crows. Maybe he is famished and cannot wait for the airlift, or maybe there is carrion on the air, and he plans to get there first.

His strange, flapping flight, much lower than a normally graceful vulture's soar, is how I feel when I am trying too hard to do something that does not quite fit me. It is a lot of work to step out of character, to do what we are not quite cut out for, to do what we really do not want to do at all. How much better to find your thermal and wing it there, dipping and soaring like this ultimate hang glider. When it is right, it looks effortless. When it does not fit, it becomes exhausting in a hurry.

I feel like that when I have to deal with too many people. I can get where I am going, all right, but *Lord* I am tired when I get there. And I am tired just watching this vulture labor to move his big, eagle-sized body in such an awkward fashion.

MAY 14 • *Sunset*

A painted turtle is bowlegging his way down the middle of Thompson Avenue. I stop, though I am in a hurry, and pick him up—the first hitch-hiker I have given in to in a long time. But this one will not be around to parade like a miniature May Day tank down this busy street if I do not. Too many people take plea-sure in target practice with any small creature in the road.

He is beautiful—liquid red-brown eyes and bright golden mark-ings on his dark carapace. I can tell he is a male from his concave plas-tron, the undershell. It helps him to stay mounted during what must surely be one of nature's most awkward acts of intercourse (love between two round rocks, or baseballs, or grapefruit).

I am surprised to see him out so late. Night is falling and like the rest of his reptilian crowd he needs the heat of the day to warm cold bones—and blood. No wonder he is hurrying down the asphalt street; he needs to get where he is going before his body slows down on him in the evening cool.

I often feel that way myself. I must accomplish this and this and this before it is too late, and my body rebels. But the asphalt is warm, like a giant solar collector, from the day's sun. It allows a later and more vigor-ous activity than is normal for a lumbering reptile who should be home in bed. Perhaps I, too, will find something to warm my cold bones and keep me going. A broad, warm road may present itself, and if it is a bit dangerous to travel, it only serves to keep the game exciting.

MAY 17 • *Night storm*

The night sky flickers like a silent movie, and I am the star in my own show. No one else is about. The storm is too far away to be audible; the action is all in the wavering, lighted screen overhead. Heat lightning, my mother used to call it.

It has been hot and humid today, and volatile; just the sort of weather that makes residents of Tornado Alley watch the sky with at least one eye as night brings cooler air, and the fronts collide with a bang. The day's heat in collision with this cooling layer makes for uncertain conditions. Cloudbursts and hail are all around us. A few tornados touch down only two counties away.

We sit on the porch swing and watch the southwestern sky. Most weather comes from just over Siloam Mountain. But stormy as it has been all around us, we remain parched. The garden soil is doing a fair imitation of the Mojave, cracked and peeling. It is ten years since the tornado banged through the edge of town, destroying two homes and damaging others. We had just signed the papers on our small Victorian house and had not yet transferred the insurance. The writhing black rope that descended from the sky to tie heaven and earth together was the most awesome thing I had ever seen—raw power, uncontrolled. It was immense as it snaked through the air. Only minutes before the sky had been broken clouds and blue. I ignored the sirens. If you live in Tornado Alley, you hear them often with no tangible results. But this thing was all

too real. We stared, transfixed, frozen in our staring, until my husband said "Let's *go*."

We had been buying groceries at the little market when we saw the unmistakable ugly smudge through the plate-glass window. I knew I did not want to be standing by that glass when it hit. A tornado has the force to drive apart the fibers of a live tree and shoot a rag into the wood like a missile.

We were miles from the farm and our familiar storm cellar. We never thought of the new house, and it was too far, in any case. We only thought that if we could get to the nearest house, perhaps they would let us shelter in their basement.

It was too late. The thing was too close. We ran across the parking lot and up the hill toward the houses, but it was almost on us. I heard the roar of the wind squeezed into painful, pulsing blasts by the wild beating of my heart loud in my ears and the silences between. I can still hear that sound if I listen hard enough.

At the last possible moment, I spotted a rift between the big lime- stone rocks on the hill. "There!" I shouted over the roar, and we dove between the rocks. A young mother and her two children had run with us. As her children cried in terror, she stood and gave us a blow-by-blow narration, "There's *no way* it can miss us. It's *coming*."

I shouted at her to get *down*, shut up, and cover her head; the flying projectiles could have gone through her body much more easily than the fibers of an oak tree.

Endless moments later, moments filled with tornado sirens, police sirens, screeching brakes, screaming people, there was silence. Dead silence. What had happened? Only hurricanes have calm centers. Had we been killed?

It had lifted. It was over. The town was safe, except for those few houses on the very edge. There were broken trees and downed power lines. Still, ten years later, I can drive out N Highway and see corrugated tin in the tops of trees, left there by that enormous wind. No lives were lost, no one was hurt. But I have never felt quite the same placid accep- tance at hearing the warning sirens.

MAY 20 • *Dawn*

Two starlings mate, silhouetted against the early morning sky. The male waves his wings as if to sweep her literally off her feet and squeals pierc- ingly—a parody of a sailor's amorous whistle. She taps him on the neck with her bill as if signaling. She certainly does not need to get his attention, it is riveted.

They are balanced precariously like a pair of impassioned tightrope walkers on the overhead lines. They mate and totter and mate again. Then the male flies off a few feet to land again on the wire. I am not the only watcher. Another male has seen the show and comes to try his luck.

The first male is having none of this competition for his chosen mate; he chases the intruder away summarily, then struts back to her, neck ruff fluffed with apparent avian pride. Big man.

It is the time to lay plans for a second family. The morning air has been crowded lately with the mechanical whirrings of a thousand baby starlings demanding breakfast, and just last night Reuben, the cat, man- aged his first kill as a three-year-old, pampered hunter of the backyards and gardens. He came home bearing the remains of a young starling, newly fledged and trying its wings. Life is as dangerous for an adolescent starling as for our own gangly offspring.

MAY 22 · *Late in the mountains*

An Ozark night is as deep as the rim of space. There is no industry, no streetlight here on the lake road to diminish the brilliance of the stars, and they decorate the domed night like jewels studding an obsidian egg by Fabergé.

I brought a pill to take; sleeping in a strange bed escapes me, and I am to judge a show tomorrow. I need to be alert, but the night is so silent, so welcoming, so magical and strange, that I choose to ignore the false sleep in a capsule and take my chances tomorrow.

I am cradled in the intermittent, repeated calls of a chuck-will's-widow outside my bedroom window. His voice is as cool as night, and I relax into it like a cherished memory. Each time he sings again I wake, and listen, and smile into the darkness. We share a peace in the night hours.

This nightjar relative of the small whippoorwill is a memory of a childhood spent as often as not in these rocky hills. He accents the first note of his call—"*chuck*-will's-widow"— in a kind of enthusiastic click; our more familiar northern Missouri whippoorwill accents the final note.

MAY 23 · *Late evening*

Two brilliant green ruby-throated hummingbirds vie for position on the feeder, pushing and shoving like kindergartners at the drinking fountain. There are three other feeder nozzles full of sweet, red nectar, but both birds seem to feel it imperative that they drink from just this *one*, and just *now*. The little birds return to the feeder again and again, hovering, flying backward and forward, wings buzzing like miniature helicopters, then zoom away to the dark, scented cedars. The sound of their rapidly beating wings seems to reverberate as I sit grinning into the dark; I think of fat, yellow bumblebees. No wonder there is a buzz of sound; tiny wings slap away at the resistant air eighty beats per second.

The hummingbirds perch like robins on the ubiquitous cedars, but very nervous robins. They pause at each perch only a few seconds before zipping away, as if the next were somehow more suitable. They are extremely active little birds. When they are not playing at their game of musical chairs in the abundant perches that surround this Ozark home, they are feeding at the garden flowers or pumping up the bright red honey and sugar-water nectar with a capillary action of their tubular tongues. Even many avid birders may not know that these tiny birds supplement their liquid diet with the protein of small insects and spiders. They use prodigious amounts of energy in constant movement. They have the highest metabolism of any warm-blooded vertebrate, with the possible exception of shrews. They *need* to feed with such concentrated attention; night is coming and they must meet their quota.

We can still see them as the light dies from the sky and the shadows under the trees deepen to black velvet. They may become torpid to conserve energy through the night if the daylight hours did not yield enough food, and if they deplete that stored in miniscule crops.

In a nearby clearing, Missouri evening primrose opens huge yellow flowers to nocturnal pollinators. It is true to its name: *Oenothera missouriensis*. *Oenothera* is Greek for "wine-scented," and this lovely, low-growing primrose of the rocky Ozark region is as sweetly scented as all the evening primrose clan. They depend on that sweet aroma to attract pollinators in the darkness. But like all evening- and night-blooming flowers, they use all the tricks in their arsenal. Their pale color helps guide insects to pollen-covered anthers, as do broad petals. Unlike the more common primrose family members that have flowers up to two inches across on tall, upright stems, Missouri evening primrose is a show-off. The lemony blooms are often nearly four inches wide. Their low-growing habit with outsized flowers reminds me of many of the plants that grow above the timberline throughout the United States. In their case, the flower is usually only normal sized. They just *look* huge when compared to stunted stems and leaves. Missouri's primrose really does have flowers as big as roses. But even on the cloudiest day, they will close by noon; they wither immediately when the sun hits them full on.

MAY 24 • *Early morning*

A waning moon hangs in the sky, almost disappearing into the early morning, faded blue. The birds have been busy for an hour, reclaiming territory from imagined intruders before the day is even officially begun. Now a ruby-throated hummingbird feeds at each red begonia in my hostess' garden, stabbing its slender beak down each flower's throat. A pair of Carolina wrens prospect for tidbits in the expensive imported top-soil around her garden plants.

(The topsoil here in the Ozarks is thin as the rose-tinted powder on my grandmother's cheek, and there is nothing but the bony rock below. If you want loam, you buy it.)

I hear a knocking on the sliding glass door. It is a young sparrow, picking at the night's contingent of insects that are flattened against the glass like wistful supplicants. I accept the unintended invitation to open the door and step out into the breaking morning.

The wildflowers are washed and glittering with dew, as if they had showered in bits of crystal and had not bothered to dry off. Downy wood mint is paler and more downy looking still with each tiny hair strung with a bead of dew.

There is a new crop of flowers here, different from our northern Missouri wildflowers. Some I recognize as old familiars, flowers that will turn up at home in a few more weeks when our more northern latitude has come as close to brushing up against summer's warm sides as this place, which nearly touches the Arkansas border. Others, I am at a loss to identify. Hardscrabble plants that seem to thrive in solid rock, they are very different from the spoiled, tender plants that luxuriate in our three-foot-deep glacial soil, soil as rich and black and aromatic as fresh coffee. Here the thin, rocky soil is stained red with iron. As a child, I always knew we had arrived in Ozark country when I saw that red earth. The wildflowers here are as hardy as the people—they have to be.

I love the sweet, slightly fishy smell of an Ozark dawn. The lake is busy with fishermen anxious to catch the day's first, and the lake roars with rush-hour traffic. Even from the road I can hear the slap of waves against the shore. I hear the thump and rumble of other boats as they pass, jarring against the liquid plaid of ten-inch wakes. It is a noisy Saturday sound at variance with the silence of the night before. The lake is a gigantic, ephemeral game of tic-tac-toe—the intersecting lines of the wakes provide a moment's play of Xs and Os.

Bobwhites call in the open woods by the road. As I round the bend I flush a pair scratching in the brick red gravel. They whir off like windup toys.

An early Eastern bluebird sits on a split-rail fence and looks at me as calmly as if I were one of the flowers that edge the road. But as I stop to observe him more closely, he recognizes me for what I am and flies, but only a few steps farther up the zig-zag fence. His nest may be nearby; bluebirds often nest along the intersections of these rough rural fences. His rusty breast matches the freshly split red cedar of the log rails, but when he turns his back to me he is wearing bright, fresh, Ozark-morning blue.

MAY 25 • *Ozark night*

There is a rustling in the brush. We hear a small thunder of feet coming at us down the tunnel of darkness beside the Osage River, along with an unnerving series of snorts and hisses and grunts. The sounds are erratic, deceptive; the creature that makes them, a mystery. Whatever is bearing down on us appears determined enough to run right up our bodies and down the other side without breaking stride. But exactly where are the sounds coming from? Which way should we go to avoid collision. And what *is* it?

A small, low-slung beast bursts from the cover of vegetation and bears down on us like traffic. "It's a skunk," Harris shouts, and with that stripe down the face I think for a moment that he is right. But the wider-than-it-is-high shape gives the creature away. This scrappy dustmop barrelling towards us is badger, not skunk, and we'd best jump one way or the other—and fast. They're not easily deterred.

We part like the Red Sea, and the badger runs between us, just where we had stood seconds before. He beats it by us in the dark and hits the clay bank like a bomb, scattering muddy shrapnel as he digs. With those strong, clawed forefeet, the badger is faster than a man with a shovel; in minutes he is gone.

Normally diurnal, these pugnacious members of the Family Mustelidae have become nocturnal where they are forced into competition with humans. This one is no exception.

Later, when the adrenalin has subsided, we take the flashlight and explore. Pigeon-toed footprints with prominent claws lead us backwards to the badger's primary den. Scattered about are the bones and hair of a hundred badger dinners, an unmistakable midden-pile of long occupation.

MAY 27 • *Predawn*

Something visits my backyard on a late-night foray; each morning the empty cat food can has been carried from the porch, where I feed the ancient outdoor cat, to the imagined safety of the grass beyond the patio. I have tried to catch the marauder in the act; I know it must be the resident opossum or the sometime raccoon—something with dextrous little hands has emptied the can of every speck of food and polished it to a metallic gleam with a thrifty tongue.

Whatever it is, the nocturnal visitor has hit us like a regular at the little café in town, every night for five nights. I have been too lazy to pick up the cans, and they are arrayed in the grass like dishes in the sink. They reproach my slothfulness while giving me much to speculate on.

What time does he come? Why do I not hear the intruder? Does he wait until the cat is finished and gone to bed in the basement before he tunes his night vision to the shine of silvery tin? Does he smell the tempting bits he will have left to him and wait in an agony of impatience for his turn? Whatever it is, it has accommodated itself well to our domestic routine; many of the wild mammals that share our territory adapt better than we do. We would scarcely know they were there in the night if it were not for the evidence of the cat food cans.

MAY 29 • *Predawn*

This morning, before the dawn, I saw the mist rising from the river between deep-green corridors of trees. It snaked pale and transparent along the twisting, sinuous shape of the creek, and I was as tempted by it as Eve by her serpent. Rising mist always calls me, an invitation to a mystery, a magical, changeling image born of warmth and coolness and moisture. Today the air is cooled by the night's rain, and the creek that has spread its shallows in the strengthening spring sun to dry is warmer by several degrees; that disparity creates magic. Droplets of water, condensed and caught up in the air as mist, are river spirit, an ectoplasmic ghost rising through the trees and gone by full sun.

But here and there rock doves punctuate that veiled illusion, visibly stirring up currents that swirl after them, and I know that a serpent spirit would not be so easily scattered. Not one as tall as two houses and as long as a river.

The temperature differential must be very slight, and my mist serpent is delicate, indeed, delicate as a dream. At the sun's first warming rays it disappears, and my temptation to follow, to enter the mist, vanishes with it.

MAY 30 • *Late evening*

The air is full of Pennsylvania fireflies sending their encoded messages of love and lust, procreation and appetite and innocence. There is something in that message that touches us—childhood's whispers on a soft spring night.

The band of small towheaded children down the street are running about my front yard. Their plastic margarine tubs replace the mason jar bug catchers I used at their age. One little blonde-haired girl—luminous in the growing darkness—is dancing like a fairy queen on my lawn, and I am thrown backward with the speed of light to nights when I, too, danced on tender May grass, blonde curls, white gown, bare feet flashing like the fireflies themselves. I am no longer the tired forty-year-old with nearsighted eyes and graying hair. I am my alter ego dancing after a magical bug to pinch off its light for a diamond with the innocent cruelty of childhood.

These children, too, gather the firefly diamonds to adorn small fat fingers, cutting short the fireflies' instinctive agenda for mating and egg-laying and new fireflies.

But even without the dangers inherent in a night populated with small children, the male firefly—not a fly at all, but a beetle family member—may meet a grisly end. The female that answers his urgent call, flashing her "why don't you come up and see me sometime" in the grass, may prefer snack to sex partner. It is a tricky business. If she is not in the mood for procreation, she will not fake a headache or flash a liberated "no" to his advances. She may simply lure him in and eat him—a good chance if she is hungry (and a *Photurus* female).

With any luck at all, though, she will

have just fed on a slug or soft-bodied mite and have something more pleasant in mind than cannibalism.

If she is a Pyralis firefly (*Photinus pyralis*) she will not eat at all in the adult form—and neither will he. These flashing meadow lights eat only in larval form.

JUNE 5 • *1:00 A.M.*

A motorcycle roars to life somewhere in the neighborhood. It drags me from sleep. It tears off a short distance, going too fast for our small-town street. The sickening skid of gravel is followed by a long, grinding shriek of metal on the pavement—then silence, a long, an endless silence. No screams, no curses, no voices. I lie there, shocked to full consciousness—surely someone must *do* something. I realize then that someone might be me. I can offer help, or a telephone for the ambulance. Bounding out of bed, grabbing robe and flashlight and glasses, I race through the house and into the street.

But there is no wreck to be seen. The silence is broken now by the voices of four or five people, some cursing, some yelling back to unseen companions. "They're all right."

Four people walk off down the street, three of them clustered protectively around the fourth, who seems to be angry—body movements rigid, abrupt, arms flailing. But the motorcycle is nowhere in sight.

A woman's voice trails after the departing quartet, "Billy, I *told* you to be careful."

I sing out into the darkness, "Everybody all right?" And receiving no answer, go back to my bed.

Adrenalin is a poor bedfellow, but I take it to my pillow, nonetheless. My heart, beating so hard it shakes my body, seems to push great pear-shaped globs of blood through my veins. I hear its pounding in my ears. My breath is shallow and irregular, as if I had run too far. Bright lights dance before my eyes when I close them, brighter than the room's normal night glow of street light and car beam.

The ancient flight-or-fight mechanism built into our genes seems to be in fine working order. The adrenalin rush would have stood me in good stead if I had had use for it.

Adrenalin is a powerful hormone, the purest found in nature. Half an ounce would be enough for the whole human race in the resting mode. Let something frighten or anger me, and that one ten billionth of an ounce of adrenalin (or epinephrin) that I store in my body, my share of the earth's half ounce, mushrooms to a ten millionth in seconds. Energy in the form of blood sugars and oxygen rushes to muscles, arming me for the proper response to emergency.

But now, when all I want is to salvage what is left of the night's sleep, the excess of powerful hormone is slow to dissipate; I awake with a start over and over throughout the night, ready to handle whatever comes. On my pillow, adrenalin serves only to keep me from sleep.

JUNE 6 • *Evening*

A sweet, remembered sound draws me into the darkness; the cricket chorus is in full voice. One particularly piercing Irish tenor of a cricket is in the garden corner. I take my flashlight to find him, but each time I come close he clams up, silent as January. At last he becomes accustomed to my light, or perhaps his ardor is so intense he can no longer be deterred by a curious naturalist. I am able to pinpoint his location by the process of elimination and the human equivalent of echolocation. He must be under that flat rock.

Indeed he is. I lift it carefully so as not to injure him, and there he sits, dark and shiny as my mother's jet beads. He jitterbugs away under the kale, indignant at the disturbance. Perhaps he will pay me back in September by crawling under my bed to sing away the night hours. "There, lady, had enough cricket music?"

JUNE 6 • *Late*

Soft wings brush my face in the dark; moths are busy in the moonlight, following pheromones.

I watched this afternoon as the cardinals tended their nestlings. The male flew to the invisible nest in the Art Nouveau trumpet vines, and the female popped out the other side as if, in some kind of Houdini magic, the bright male had become a dun-colored female.

But moments later, apparently after checking on the young, he, too, popped back out to sit nearby, chirping loudly. At first I imagined him remiss in his duty but then realized that the female is so camouflaged on the nest as to disappear into the tangled dun of old vines and branches. The male is visible as a stoplight.

Now, after dark, I check to make sure she has returned safely. Even in the beam of my flashlight it is almost impossible to differentiate her from the surroundings. She stares back at me, round black eye unblinking, and I excuse myself, embarrassed at my intrusion in a private family moment. These most common backyard birds still have their secrets.

JUNE 8 • *5:15 A.M.*

Birds wear away the last of the night with their territorial arias, slowly fading the featureless black to blue velvet and indigo and stone-washed denim and chambray.

Shapes begin to stand out again from the flat, cookie-cutter stage set of night. Light defines form, accentuates volume, explains texture. The blue-gray shapes, at first stamped out of monochromatic sameness, take on reality as if life were ballooned into them. They become languidly rounded, they take on depth and dimension.

I watch until hunger drives me to my sensuous, ritualistic June breakfast. The red mulberry tree calls like voodoo, and the taste of the fat, oval berries forms itself in my mouth like the shapes of morning, round and distinct and sweet, before I ever make the first move. Each day since the first berry ripened on the volunteer tree I take my leave to the mulberry festooned with dark offerings. I never tire of that taste, with its barest hint of wildness. Unlike the blackberries ripening in the woods, which bite back with strong, feral flavor, these berries are sweet as home. Bland, some describe them, but if I am careful to pick an occasional red-black oval just on its way to fullness, I can spike the bland with tart-sweet goodness.

I share my morning ritual with the resident robin, who works the top of the tree while I ply the lower branches. There is plenty for both of us, but he bitterly resents the intrusion. After all, he—or a member of his clan—planted this volunteer manna in the first place. A bird has his rights. It is his inheritance, and he puts pretenders in their places.

He *perps* indignantly at me through a huge berry. It is comical to see that the fruit, proportionately so large in the scissors of his bill, in no way diminishes his ability to scold—loud and clear!

June 8 • *Late*

The house is still and airless at 3:00 A.M. I cannot get my breath. It feels as if all the oxygen has been used up by the occupants—human and feline. There is none of the fresh night air of outdoors in this motionless atmosphere. I flip on the attic fan to draw the night inside, and freshness rushes toward me, past me, up my body and out the fan-powered vent on the ceiling. I am in a cool river of oxygen. I swim in delight and breathe the river like a fish.

Why is it the night house in winter never has this choking closeness, this deadness, this stillness? The furnace circulates the same stale night air. Why don't I gasp like a beached fish in February? A midwestern summer is not a pleasant thing. I endure it, but with rancor.

JUNE 9 • *9:30 P.M.*

The changing of the guard on a small-town street: it is a swirling cloud of chimney swifts forming and reforming over the ancient smokestack like leaves caught in a tornado. And like leaves they fall into the open mouth of the stack, fluttering—five, ten, twenty at a pass. Or change their minds at the last second, chittering away from the gaping hole back into the cloud of birds that moves first east, then west, then back to center.

There are thousands of them, all chittering wildly like mad flying mice and punctuated by the larger forms of nightjars with their harsh voices. I try to pick these out from their smaller cousins by sight alone, but the swirling mass of birds is too confusing. I spin like a centrifuge trying to keep it in sight, sorted out and sensible.

The moon, pink as a sodium streetlight through the soft blue cushion of clouds, silhouettes the smokestack. I find my father's night glasses in the trunk of the car and stand transfixed as the fluttering forms of the swifts drop from the sky. But at last they are gone. The sky is empty except for the nightjars. The changing of the guard is complete.

JUNE 10 • *Evening*

The female cardinal has abandoned her nest. Perhaps the hard rain last night finished it, but there was only one sickly chick in the nest two days ago, and a stench and buzz of flies. Tonight there is nothing. My flashlight finds only an empty collection of grass and twigs and shreds of plastic. An empty nest is a broken promise: sad and irredeemable.

A single lightning bug visits my back screen, blinking his cold neon message at me as he crawls up the door. Then bang, he drops like a stone. The female usually lays low in the grass. Did he get an offer he could not refuse from the weeds by the porch?

Tonight the abandoned garden is alight with dozens of moving lights like small friendly stars come for a visit. Beyond my fence the slow dance goes on in the warm darkness—up, down, and gently up again to the very tops of the oak trees on the hill. If this were Malaysia, the fireflies might congregate in a single tree to blink in unison their message of love and procreation.

JUNE 11 · *Late*

The waxy blossoms of yucca shine in the darkness like earthbound galaxies; they are spread out along their stalks like the long swath of the Milky Way. They are pure white, untouched by pink or yellow and I would expect them to attract night moths seeking their nectar, but nothing disturbs their repose.

One stalk is so heavy with blooms it has fallen of its own weight. The air is thick and sweet with scent, accentuated by the welcome cool of the evening, sweet as dreaming.

I drink it in gratefully. It was a long, hot afternoon, nearly ninety-five degrees and humid. I sat under the redbud tree with a damp towel draped around my neck so I could stand to be outdoors in such pounding heat. Now that the sun has fallen behind the rim of trees, the air is cool enough to breathe once more. I suck it in greedily, starved for its cool sweetness. I will sleep tonight.

A whippoorwill still sings in the woods, a sweet accompaniment to sleep, though I would expect the time for territorial calling to be long past. These secretive birds, seldom seen in daylight, seem to exult in singing for its own sake.

I have looked for their camouflaged forms on the ground in the daytime, or for their streamlined shapes plastered tight to a low branch. Their small, weak feet cannot perch solidly, and they take advantage of their coloring to pass for the proverbial bump on a log. They sit tight lengthwise on a limb, blending with dun-colored branches and twigs. So invisible are they that walkers have been known to step on them in the forest.

I have seen their eyes glow like the eyes of cat in the light of a strong beam as they hunt for insects on the wing. They may not be strong perchers but they are most excellent gleaners of the airways. One might almost suspect them of the talents of echolocation like a bat, but more likely that huge, gaping beak is just very efficient at vacuuming the air for moths and other wingers.

JUNE 12 • *3:20 A.M.*

The neighbor's dog shatters my sleep like broken glass. He repeats his lament over and over. I can see him with muzzle uplifted to the moon in earnest entreaty, as if he would call it down.

I am angry and tense. *Damn* that dog, why doesn't someone *do* something? I am angrier with his owners, who care nothing for his howling. But at last I pretend he is a wolf, instead, a natural, wild sound, and I am able to blend into his song like white shapes in the long arctic night. Why is it that when it is my neighbor's dog I am irritated beyond measure at the inconsideration of humans, but when I conjure up the audible wraith of wolf I sleep undisturbed?

It is work maintaining the charade. My concentration wavers now and then, and a power surge of irritation returns. But at last I convince myself those wavering howls are wolf, not husky. I can sleep in wildness.

JUNE 13 • *Night*

It is 3:00 A.M. and I am dragged from sleep by an odd peeping outside my bedroom window. Fuzz, the stray tom, is on the killing fields he has chosen for reasons known only to himself. Here he has dispatched mice, shrews, and baby birds, shattering my repose with death. I repeat platitudes about feline instincts to myself until the killing is over.

Unless I can stop it. This night the sound is too strange. I intervene. It is an Eastern cottontail, perhaps a month old, making this odd sound, unlike a rabbit's quavering scream. The guilty cat drops it and runs at my approach. I can find no wound, the tiny bit of sentient life lies stunned in my hand, unmoving. The only solution I can find at this hour is to put him in a cage and shut him in the garden shed until morning. If he lives, I will take him to Pete Rucker, the veterinarian who seems to inherit all the injured wild things. Last year he successfully raised a fawn that had a run-in with a sickle. The vet speaks with certain affection for Tiffany, the three-legged deer that still haunts his country place.

JUNE 14 • *Early*

Green mounds of trees take on form and shape in the warming light of early morning, like muffins rising in the oven. The light is poured, buttery, over their sides, throwing shadows in deep relief.

The air still smells of night, sweet and rich with leaves and loam and mycelium, but warming and drying now, becoming lighter in scent as well as in the visual light of the strengthening sun.

The world makes itself new each morning from the promises of night and the memory of yesterday. I feel this small piece of earth I stand on turning to the sun, turning to face the day. A yeastiness rises in me as well, a bubbling. It will be a fine day.

JUNE 15 • *Early evening*

The cicadas are back. That loud, metallic buzzing, rising and falling and rising again, over and over, says summer. I am a child again, looking for their empty, discarded hulls like blown amber. I watch as a stiff-moving

amber bug perambulates up my herb garden Saint Francis. He reaches the perfect place for metamorphosis, or perhaps he can simply wait no longer. He stops and seems to gather strength within himself. A split opens at the broad bison shoulder of the bug, opens and widens and becomes a vertical slash through which the insect emerges. He seems to swell out of his rigid husk like bread dough in the warm summer night; he is pale like dough, as well.

At last he is free of the confines of his chitinous carapace. He steps out of it like a forgotten life and flexes the promise of his new self, testing his boundaries. His wings, damp and crumpled like a used tissue, straighten and unfold. They are lovely with their finely drawn network of black lines and cellophane sails.

He takes on color from within. His paleness is replaced by rich greens and browns and blacks. Now he is fully formed and ready to take his place in the loud alleluia chorus.

JUNE 15 • *Late*

We could find only a broken foreleg on the tiny Eastern cottontail; no way to set a bone as small as a toothpick. Pete suggested I keep the little rabbit confined for ten days and perhaps it would heal sufficiently to allow it to survive, like Tiffany. But now, before I sign off for the night, I find that the tomcat has claimed a belated victim. The rabbit has succumbed to the trauma of being mauled—and of being held captive, even if for his own good. It is a rare thing to raise one of these fragile little creatures; they are the essence of wildness for all their cuddly vulnerability. They do not emerge unscathed from run-in with a cat *or* a human with any regularity.

MIDSUMMER

The Shortest Nights

HEAT AND HUMIDITY ARE THE WATERMARKS of a Midwestern summer, not an arbitrary date on the Gregorian calendar. Not even the summer solstice, when the shortest nights of the year are packed tightest with life, marks the true beginning of summer—or its middle, for that matter. Earth's syncopated rhythms have little enough to do with the numbers.

Midsummer's Night holds its own special magic close to its vest like a card shark with a winning hand. In folklore, in literature, in imagination, it plays its cards with cunning and delight. We are unendingly surprised. There may be fools wearing asses' heads about—there may be fairies. On *this* night it is fair to suspend disbelief and celebrate the fullness of the season.

June 21—Midsummer's Night, the summer solstice—may usher in official summer with all the heraldry of Titania's antic court, but here in the heartland, true summer comes when it will. We may have a chilly June, more like March than the long hot days we expect. We may have August-like weather. July is as inconstant.

True summer—the glowing red middle of the season—comes when the wind blows hot, when humidity hangs heavy over the hills at dawn like a damp blanket, when dusk brings slight relief from the sultry, soggy day.

Dew beads at each leaf margin at daybreak; I am soaked to the knee before I walk ten feet.

Summer storms may be more bluster than bite. Towering cumulus clouds bully their way into the upper atmosphere. They can threaten all they want, but often they simply move on, muttering to themselves and leaving hard, cracked earth. Dew may be the only moisture we see, and it is welcome.

But all this airborne moisture is magic; it pulls tricks impossible in dryer climates. Hills are like stage sets behind their veils of humidity, progressively paler and more featureless, flat as cardboard. Fingers of mist trail up the valleys and rise on summer nights as if wakening over cool, still ponds. Fireflies are like fox fire in this unearthly, no, this most wonderfully *earthly* mist.

Insects—katydids, crickets, dusk-singing cicadas—drill through our brains with their raucous night music, avid for a mate. I marvel that they have time to eat; many do not in their adult form. Their sole function is this: singing and mating and the laying of a million tiny eggs.

Killdeer are nesting in the Rose Moon, hiding their rock-colored eggs among the gravel in bowl-shaped scrapes. You will not find a killdeer begging for nesting materials. She makes do with the earth itself.

Many birds have begun second families. Black rat snakes search for them in the dusk. These familiar garden snakes are commonly diurnal, but hot summer nights allow the hunt to stretch long into the evening, like the party at the next campsite. Cold blooded snakes absorb the sun's heat and convert it on the spot to the energy it is. They hunt as long as they are warm enough. And hungry enough.

Sounds are loud on a midsummer night, or perhaps it is only that I am more likely to be there to hear them as I seek relief from the growing heat. Dusk does promise respite, though it sometimes reneges, and the sullen sultriness lasts through the small hours. By morning I am drained, exhausted by the effort to breathe.

But more often there *is* relief to be found. The nights may be short, but they are julep sweet, cool and refreshing with a sprig of mint. We share them with the birds and mammals, reptiles and amphibians that are naturally nocturnal as well as those that look, as we do, for a bit of cool. Night is never more welcome.

JUNE 16 • *Predawn*

Morning comes too early. It is dark as night when I tumble out of bed at 5:45 A.M., at least in the house. The sky has begun to wash its Japanese indigo to pale cobalt in the east.

My eyelids are swollen; they open only reluctantly. My legs feel as if they weigh a hundred pounds apiece. My body has the familiar ache that getting up produces, not an ache of age or arthritis, nothing so serious as all that. Just morning, and too early.

A morning without coffee is no morning at all; call if off, it does not exist. I cannot cope.

But what makes us think we like this bitter brew, this South American tyrant? I opened a fresh can last night, my favorite brand—a mixture of lovely, toasted coffee beans from the high mountains of Columbia and the rich Louisiana chicory root. The scent, the aroma was exquisite. I could get no more pleasure from a rose. Odd to think that the chemical compounds related to that pungent fragrance are the result of destruction, the breaking down of the bean itself in the roasting.

JUNE 17 • *Early*

You need gills to survive a Midwestern summer. The air itself is blue with moisture, heavy with its weight of water. I swim through it, pushing my way forward as though in the deep pool in the creek, and it feels thick, viscous, resisting my passage.

The trees on the hill are blue, the veil of moisture is visible even in the early dawn light. Later, as the sun begins to tint the edges of the sky with pink, aquamarine is tinged with shimmering, iridescent color—blue, violet, peach, lavender.

My sandals were damp and unpleasant when I slipped them on this morning. The attic fan pulls in the welcome cool of night, but also the pervasive wet. In my studio office, envelopes seal themselves in stacks and stamps lick themselves prematurely. I keep them now between sheets of waxed paper. My empty popcorn bowl is lined with a thin film of water. A miniature pool of brine lines at the bottom; the salt has attracted moisture all night long.

I left a load of clothes drying on the line until bedtime, but "drying" should wear quotation mark fences to keep it from any semblance of reality. They hang as limp and damp as when I put them there hours before, despite the long hot afternoon to dry.

You could not *buy* a breeze this morning. I could be looking at a still photograph if it were not for the dawn chorus of birds and our eyes' talent for depth perception. The only moving air is outside my neighbor's air conditioner, left on all night for the comfort of a visiting grandmother. The hot exhaust stirs the elm sprouts beside her window unit in a parody of a morning breeze.

JUNE 18 • *Late evening*

The songbirds form an angry lynching party and come gunning for our owl tape. They flock from the surrounding forest, scolding, strident. The noise becomes almost too loud—jangling. I become as tense as the threatened birds. Jays, crows, robins, chickadees, titmice—all screaming avian curses and threats. This small-town park ain't big enough for all of us, pardner.

What have we wrought with our play of owl calls at the edge of the woods? We had expected to call up the territorial barred owl who owns the hill, but we arrived just as the crepuscular light was beginning its long slide into darkness. The feathered vigilantes are still on patrol, and vigilant.

But the sound seems much too localized, too frantic to be a response to taped owl calls. There must be the real thing about after all.

And there is. Scanning the wall of trees that butt solidly up to our tiny clearing I find the warm brown shape of an enormous owl against that unvaried green. He has chosen a clear field of vision on a dead limb and disregards totally the brouhaha his presence has stirred. He must have winged in silently to find what was muscling in on his territory. He does not bother to answer; we are no more a threat to him than the sleepy songbirds that will soon give up their mobbing and return to night perches. If it had been full daylight, and we had interrupted his hard-earned sleep with our canned conversation, he might have been more concerned.

He needs his daytime rest now that he is feeding his bottomless adolescent nestlings; barred owls may have to fill up to five mouths with a never-ending procession of small prey. Unless one or more of the nestlings themselves become the entrée, that is. Like many birds of prey, owls' eggs hatch in the order in which they are laid rather than all incubating at once. That means the youngest owl is also the smallest and weakest. If prey is scarce he may die from malnutrition or be eaten by his older siblings.

We have intrigued him with our wild mix of great horned, screech and, more urgently requiring his attention, barred owl calls. He stares unblinking, not even swivelling his head to anticipate his small attackers. Then, at last (and just as I retrieve my binoculars to stare back at him with my own big round eyes) he lifts off and flies low over us on soundless wings and on across the creek, all in one smooth, unflapping glide. I see his outstretched primaries (two lost in molt) and his barrel-chested body like a flying nail keg. Talons are tucked in tight for his aerodynamic flight.

Are our owl calls so sickly sounding after all? Three very late turkey vultures risk a late evening flyby just overhead on the rapidly cooling thermals. Do we sound like a parliament of injured Strigidae?

They check us out once, twice, three times, spiraling lower each time as if gravity played as big a part as curiosity. I begin to fantasize taking cover—hit the dirt! But the final flyby seems to have satisfied them. Reconnaissance mission complete; we are not edible. Yet. They sail languidly toward night roosts, their black bodies blending into the growing shadows like night itself.

JUNE 19 • *Early*

In the early morning light—cool, like water—we stand by the drying creek. It is dying for lack of rain. The banks crack like chapped lips, and an opaque scum covers the surface, sealing it from edge to edge. The water gasps for breath, turning green and sour.

In a shrinking pool just past the twisted oak that grips the limestone bed with its toes, a hundred water striders are stranded like sailors in a strange port. They stand around and talk at the edges of the pool, complaining about the lack of water.

They are contentious creatures, normally, territorial and fierce competitors for food. But now they skim slowly over the thickening surface of the pool, squeezing together, bumping shoulders—desultory. They watch the sky for rain and pray for moving water and a way out.

I can inspect them closely here, where they have nowhere to go. Those widespread legs skate almost effortlessly over the water on the molecule-thick surface film; an insect waterproofing keeps them from sinking. They scull from one end of the pool to the other, their feet dimpling the surface as they hunt for aquatic larvae or flying insects that may have fallen into the water. In the South, they are called "Jesus Bugs," tribute to their walking on water.

At this close range I can see the white stripes on their sides. Beneath each strider this white is repeated in reflection—where there is clear enough water to reflect at all.

JUNE 21 • *Midsummer's Night*

Troll, fairies, wood sprites. This night hike at the Martha Lafite Thompson Nature Sanctuary is different from all other hikes of the year. It winds through an enchanted wood of troll holes and tree spirits, past the fireflies' slow, syncopated dance to the music that drifts through the trees. The hair rises on my arms; it's pure delight, not fear.

But a thrill of childish anxiety surfaces when the troll makes his appearance. He rises, bearded and stinking, dressed in a coyote skin, from beneath his bridge and demands payment for our passage. Be it barter or flesh—he doesn't care which. We hide the succulent young children, who squeal in mock fear, and offer linden-tree berries. He accepts with a glower. "It's not a free bridge, you know, it's a *troll* bridge."

Down the luxuriant, mossy path, we leave offerings for more benign beings under the bending, listening trees. Small, papery lanterns, the fruit of the bladderpod bush—pale green relatives of the domestic Chinese Lantern plant—are placed in a circle for the fairies.

These small beings love circles; you may have come across a ring of mushrooms in the wood, chairs tiny enough, at last, for the fairies to hold their board meetings. Later, when we return, the bladderpods are large and lit. We can just see a circle of white-clad creatures down the tunnel, but we are not allowed to pass this way again. It's a closed meeting; no Sunshine Law applies to fairy confabs, not on Midsummer's Night.

I feel like a child again on this special night. I step outside my adult persona and am free to feel the wonder like any of the children who walk with us. It is a gift from the nature sanctuary staff to all of us.

JUNE 23 • *Night*

A summer thunderstorm grumbles sullenly in the night sky, threatening reprisals. I wonder if it will really rain this time, really get serious. I smell the rain in the air. The sky flashes with intermittent lights.

The clouds look red, lit up by streetlight and lightning bolts. A long, slow bolt reaches halfway across the sky, twisting back on itself, writhing in pain like an injured snake.

A raindrop strikes my hand, another plops onto my page. The air is fresher, at last, and easier to breathe.

The wind rises, lifts my wind sock and twists it, then whirls it around like a bright dancer. The small, stiff leaves on our young poplar tree dance, too, in short, staccato steps—tap dancing with the lightning. Their polished surfaces catch fire with each flash and semaphore a cryptic message. I feel cool rain on my bare feet.

The storm is only a tease, after all. Nothing much happens. A few stomach growls in the clouds, a few lovely pink streaks of lightning, the cool shower, and then it is over.

JUNE 26 • *Night*

Strange, soft noises tonight. There are the normal insect songs, of course, and the metallic cry of a nighthawk, but also these: a clicking whispering; a soft snorting; a rhythmic hissing; the rattling sound of claws on a hard surface, just barely audible.

I fetch the flashlight to play Sherlock. The clicking is the sound of paper wasps, still active on their cellulose nest at 11:00 P.M. They crawl over the hexagonal chambers with a dry whisper.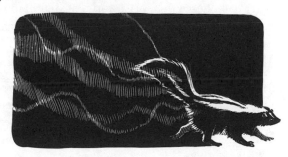

The hissing in the tree turns out to be the amorous tomcat and his heavy breathing; apparently the young female stray is in heat. I try to coax her down to feed her, but she is deliciously afraid, coy like a young girl on her first date. She pleads fear of heights, though she is only two feet above the top of the wooden fence and only inches out of my reach. The tom is on the limb above her, snorting lasciviously like Pan.

And finally I follow the soft ticking to the cave formed by the legs of our storage cabinet on the back porch. The opossum has camped out there, waiting for our ancient cat to finish his dinner. I can see the moist shine of his pink nose and his soft, silver-tipped fur in my flashlight beam. It is his rhythmic scratching that makes the ticking sound.

A scent of skunk is in the air. The neighborhood dogs catch it in their sensitive nostrils, roll it around on their tongues and wail pitiably in anticipation of disaster. And disaster it would be. These well-armed nocturnal creatures in dapper black and white carry munitions, and they know it. They are cocky. Mess with me, and you will regret it.

Our old Siamese found out where his own limitations were—or should have been—just this side of confrontation with an Eastern skunk. He hightailed it in—a pitiful, wet, stringy, slimy ball of misery. His face was laced with a web of skunk spray. His eyes were stung shut.

JUNE 27 • *3:00 A.M.*

An early morning rainstorm calls me out to close the car windows. When I went to bed the sky was deep velvet; not a cloud masked the sprinkle of stars.

This was a polite shower, shy and self-effacing. No lightning flashes called attention, no drum roll—just a gentle rain.

It was a lovely time to be about. Shadows moved in the street. Little brown bats gleaned the air around the streetlight, their flittering flight an aerial "kissing cousin" to that of chimney swifts. I hear an occasional soft cry and take my night glasses to the porch to watch them feed.

They are amazing little hunting machines. They take no handicap for darkness. A close-up view of those big, naked ears tells me why. Each ear

is ridged with sound catchers that funnel information downward to the bat's brain. He acts on it instantly, turning in perfect precision with the flight of his insect prey. I stood barefoot in the rain to watch.

Two years ago a tiny bat got inside my neighbor's window screen and was stuck there between the screen and the glass. By morning he was dead—of fright? She called me over to identify the body. It was miniature, just over three inches long. His head was about a half an inch long, with ears that long again, at least.

The leatherlike wings were bent back upon themselves and at the first joint was a small, sharp claw. The translucent leather of the wings contrasted oddly with the fine, soft fur of the rest of his body. I blew into the delicate nap on his back. At the base the fur was nearly black, but the outer half of each hair was a warm, medium brown. The ombre of his coloring was quite beautiful, and I mourned his small passing.

JULY 1 • *Evening*

The neighborhood watch of songbirds sounds the alarm. Their mixed cries are astonishingly loud, and I cannot ignore them any longer. At first I can see only the wall of green leaves and an occasional noisy, flying shape. But as I watch, they point out the direction of their concern like feathered arrows.

It is a black rat snake again. He is far overhead this time—twenty-five feet up and twined around a slender limb like a vine. His sense of smell must be honed to a fine point to have found the nest so high overhead in the slippery elm tree. Or has he watched from the woodpile the comings and goings of the parent birds? Even I did not know the nest was there, tucked in the limbs over the chair where I sit to write and dream and drink my coffee. A predator's sensory awareness is impressive. And this one, at least, always seems to get hungry at dusk.

The chickadees keep their distance—barely—as if aware of their small vulnerability. They are an easy target for the snake. The jays and robins are more aggressive, but the mockingbird is oddly silent and only just visible in the tangle of green. Perhaps they have no alarm call in that incredible repertoire. I crane my neck to see him better. Yes, it is a mockingbird, streamlined, elegant—and silent.

The wrens are a constant Scottish burr of sound. They dart in for a quick jab and, just as quickly, dart back.

I watch in dismay as the snake moves slowly, hypnotically toward the nest, eyes unblinking, attention fastened unwavering on his objective. The robins must be the parent birds; they are most aggressive in trying to draw his attention or to dislodge him entirely. But he is most firmly braced. I can see his sinuous blackness wrapped around the slender branch, muscular loops braced against nearby twigs. He is single-minded in his mission and not about to fall.

I fantasize throwing a rock at him, but know I could never aim so well. I fantasize shooting him, but know I would hit a bird instead, or the nest. I like rat snakes. I admire their glossy scales and aerial acrobatics. I know they must eat, and I do not begrudge them this—but not robin eggs and not right over my head.

I am trapped and mesmerized, helpless as he enters the waiting bowl of the songbirds' nest and eats the tiny blue eggs, one by one. I can hear them crack—a small ticking sound—each time he takes another. Damn. Three. Four. How many must he have?

Minutes later it is silent. He is finished. The nest is empty, and he is in victorious retreat. The neighborhood watch is disbanding; there is nothing left here to protect.

And just as full dark falls I step out to look again for the nest high overhead. Only the parent robin hops disconsolately back and forth now. The defenders have left. The snake is elsewhere, digesting the rich protein of his prey. The robin hops again and again to the nest, chirping in alarm, and looks into the empty bowl as if in disbelief. Anthropomorphism is out of favor among serious naturalists, but anyone who has ever lost can recognize this unbelieving return, time and again, this anguished *perping*. I am desolate for her. Life and death is an everyday part of a naturalist's world, but this was somehow too close to home. This was *my* territory. I feel as violated as the robin's nest, and as empty.

JULY 7 • *Night*

The pregnant moon drags herself up later and later as she nears full term. Tonight moonrise is slower by nearly a half an hour.

Yes, the moon is slow; yet the katydid's antic songs come faster and faster in staccato repetitions. Frantic and comical, they build to a climax that never comes. They wind me tight as a clock, expecting the explosion.

I wander in the night, unable to sleep, and find a fellow prowler in

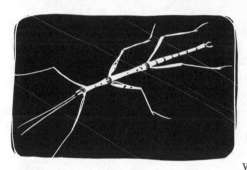

the dark. A giant walkingstick, nearly six inches long, is awake and hunting for prey. During the day he lies low; wearing his most excellent disguise, he is well hidden from predatory birds. He looks exactly like a glossy young twig even to the fine details of "new growth" and coloring. I would not be surprised to watch him sprout a fresh green leaf.

I have heard the rainlike patter of walkingstick eggs falling to earth on a summer night. I have seen the miniscule young toddling all over the woods—half-inch long, thready green twiglets that tickle my arms when I sit to read beneath the redbud tree.

JULY 9 • *Night*

There will be a record low temperature tonight; already it is down to just below sixty degrees. If I did not know by the big thermometer on the shed—or by my deliciously cool skin—I could tell by the songs of crickets and katydids. The crickets are slower, and there are fewer of them singing. But the katydids really tell the tale. Their rackety notes are half an octave lower and much slower than normal. They sound like some odd kind of tropical night bird, not like familiar night-calling insects at all. When the insect calls slow and thin and deepen until there are no more left, the hint is fall.

Amazing how loud a single insect can be when he sends his insistent mating call into the cool night air. I wonder what the decibel level is. Not, surely, as piercing as on a hot, humid night. These evoke a lazy, laid-back mood, a mating call by the coolest of the cool. "Hey-y-y, baby."

I would wonder that the female katydid could even recognize this long, low call as the male of her own species. But scientists believe night callers take their own body temperature into account when interpreting mating signals—if she is cold, so is he.

Even the trilling of the toads is subdued. Tonight I can hear only one or two over at the edge of the abandoned garden. These small amphibians are cold-blooded; they need the warmth of summer nights to sing, and tonight is just too cold.

It will be a good night for sleeping. The cool air comes in my northern bedroom window, washing me like a stream. The full moon is past, and the sky is dark and transparent, with stars layered in the deep like fish in the sea. The house is cradled, rocked in the wide swath of the Milky Way and the sweet, cool songs of toads and insects.

JULY 14 • *Nightfall*

Dusk is achingly beautiful, pure as first love. Night is just tipping over the last of the day like the cover on a rolltop desk. A small rim of blue light hangs suspended in the west. All the rest of the sky is rich cobalt—glistening, trembling, transparent.

Smudges of artist's charcoal suggest low clouds dark against the western glow. High in the sky, lighter clouds are reversed, as if someone had lifted them out of a rich watercolor wash with a damp tissue. And high overhead the first pinpricks of light pierce the blueness as the stars appear tentatively, one by one. Soon they will own the night by strength of numbers alone. The moon rises later and later, offering scant competition. I will not be up to see it bob from behind the far trees, gold turning silver in the sky. The moon keeps its own odd schedule, independent of daybreak and nightfall.

Only the nightjars ply the cobalt sky, bent scimitar wings slicing the night to pieces. Their metallic cries are a harsh counterpoint to the chimeral loveliness; they call me back to earth.

JULY 15 • *Night*

The hot night air is thick with sound and humidity and the scent of leaves drying to a heady potpourri.

The roselike scent is stronger at night; by daylight I investigate the source with my pocket microscope. The elm tree is being attacked by tiny beige bugs with black-spotted bodies. They are the larvae of oak lace bugs. In their wake they leave hundreds of tiny black spots on the leaves and a fine, furry webbing. They are the locus of the sweet, dry scent. Like aphids, they make a kind of honeydew.

The dying leaves look lightly peppered with their droppings. Adult oak lace bugs stay nearby as if out of parental concern. Although they are supposed to prefer the tree that gives them their name, they seem quite at home in the elm.

JULY 16 • *Early*

An early morning walk through the park brings many more sightings of wildlife than usual. In the growing, crepuscular light, the guard changes. Nocturnal creatures are heading home to their dens and perches after a long night. We see the barred owl zeroing in on his nest tree and imagine a certain weary slump to his measured wingbeats.

The deer snort in alarm as they discover us about so early. They are used to having these hours to themselves. We watch their white flags bounding up the hill like disembodied lights, fox fire in the dimness.

Rabbits are out in small feeding squads, eating the tender dewy tips of grasses—food and drink at the same time. In the short half mile of park road, we spot four sets of big ears swivelling to pick up the sound of our approach, four white tails bobbing like will-o'-the-wisps against the dark-shadowed edge of the woods. One cottontail, younger and bolder than the rest, sits unperturbed by our nearing. He is far more interested in his meal. We are within six feet of him and still he continues to eat. His hunger must outstrip his fear by a length. We see the white flash of his eye, but he will not be deterred. He has one long and particularly desirable stem in his mouth that we watch disappear. It grows shorter and shorter like a strand of spaghetti, seedy and wobbling slightly as it is chewed. We do not have the heart to disturb him further and turn back the way we came, leaving him in peace. I look back over my shoulder to find him rapidly dispatching another seed-tipped stem with apparent satisfaction. It must taste all the sweeter served up with relief.

JULY 17 • 3:00 A.M.

The temperature has not dropped much below eighty degrees, and the still air feels much warmer out of doors than it does inside. The artificial wind manufactured by the attic fan makes it seem about seventy degrees.

Outside, it is perfect weather for mosquitoes. But this night I do not stay out long enough for them to follow the carbon-dioxide highway of my breath back to my tempting expanse of flesh. A July nightgown does not cover a lot, and the threat of a dozen itchy "bites" bothers me considerably. Mosquito bites are fierce itchers. Each time one of these blood-sucking little females inserts that specialized, barbed proboscis beneath unwilling skin, she injects a powerful irritant, one that seems to have an interminable shelf life.

Itching is the least of our concerns. Mosquitoes carry not only malaria and yellow fever, but human and equine encephalitis, dengue fever, filariasis, and dog heartworm—this last, of course, of more concern to the family dog and his owners.

I cannot bear to coat my already sticky skin with repellant. It is a last resort, a last-ditch defense as far as I am concerned. My backyard sojourn is short. Bed calls, and my pillow by the open window is the only cool spot in town, if I turn it often enough.

Tomorrow, in the light, I will inspect the neighborhood for prime mosquito larvae areas. The birdbath needs changing, the cat dish, too, but discarded tin cans and old tires beyond the abandoned garden are more likely nurseries. Some mosquitoes even prefer these man-made egg-laying sites to natural ones, and a few species may even enter our houses by choice to lay their eggs in vases of flowers.

JULY 19 • Night

My flashlight is a cartoon laser sword in the thick, humid air. I can see it sweeping the night before me, an opaque column of light.

I came out to inspect the spiders' webs. The grass spider by the porch sits waiting for prey to pass by, its funnel web at the ready. I can see the web's architect crouched deep within the funnel. Its eyes reflect my flashlight beam with a tiny, green glow.

The garden cart is firmly tied to the rotary cultivator by an immense silvery orb. The web is empty. I see three large holes in the disc; it must have barely slowed down insects too strong to fall prey to the orb weaver. Neatly wrapped in one corner of the sticky net that was extruded from the spider's own protein, a meal awaits. It is a tight little package, stunned but not killed—fresh protein to replenish her supply—the spider's equivalent of home canning, I suppose.

I tickle the web with a blade of grass to see if I can raise the weaver. Sure enough, after a moment or two, a spiny Micrathena comes to investigate. She has hidden at the end of one of the supporting girders, waiting for the vibration that signals another hapless blunderer. Her large, spiny abdomen is impressive; she must be a fearsome sight as she approaches her prey.

In a corner of her web is a smaller, messier construction. It looks very much like a baby black and yellow *Argiope* spider, the kind that weave bold white ladders into their webs, but the web itself is not right. It is an untidy net of short, connecting strands in no particular order or design. Perhaps its owner is a small "bowl and doily" spider, or an *Argyrode*. These often share webs—and prey—with larger spiders.

Sheet web spiders have slung their hammocks between the woodpile and the grass. Everywhere my flashlight beam falls, I see more evidence of my backyard jungle, where everything is out to eat everything else. I am grateful to have gotten over my unreasoning terror of spiders.

JULY 20 • *Sunset*

The setting sun is a glowing copper coin in the pale sky. All day the sun was overlaid with a veil of pale white. An overcast of thinnest cloud coupled with 80 percent humidity has worn away the blue summer sky almost to white. Now, at sunset, a third of that pale sky is tinted with peach, and the remainder is, at last, blue. The overcast is sliding over the edge of the world, dragged off into the lair of the westering sun.

The spiny Micrathena has rebuilt her web for the night's hunt. It is as perfect as a phonograph record. The carefully preserved prey has been consumed, and by all evidence, digested. Last night the spider's spiny abdomen was distended, glossy; she had eaten well. Tonight she has a lean and hungry look about her. Her abdomen appears to have shrunken in on itself to just over half of last night's size. It has lost its stretched, silky gloss, as well. The lines that marked it at regular intervals now almost touch. She needs that well-set trap.

Already she has caught two tiny flying insects—hardly enough to satisfy that half-inch abdomen of hers. I wonder how much of it is stomach? The small web sharer has been joined by another, perhaps a mate. It is slightly smaller. These have attached their messy web more tightly to the guy wires securing the orb and wait for dinner to arrive.

JULY 22 • *Twilight*

Dusk stretches out its allotted time jealously, as if reluctant to give up the day. Except in the west, where a roseate stain lingers, the sky has turned gray blue.

Around the perimeter of the big lake, whippoorwills call to each other, as if singing out a neighborly "hi." The nocturnal birds fill the summer nights of my memory with the sweetest songs of all, and the most insistent. Tonight's singers, however, are remarkably restrained. One repetitious Missouri bird called over two thousand times before his distraught listener made a beeline for his liquor cabinet to numb his senses.

A flock of geese down by the dam takes momentary wing, complaining loudly at being disturbed by a passing johnboat. They rise a few feet above the dusky lake, swing in a wide, slow arc, and drop again, one by one. I hear them chattering comfortably as they settle in for the night, offshore and safe from predatory mammals.

The air is soft as a breath. The wind has come up just enough to cool my July skin. I feel as if I have slipped on a loose satin gown, as if its cool, rich folds have settled lightly against my bare skin.

The land is dark. The hills have melded into a solid, smoky mass. But the water and the sky are slow to part with the light. They speak to each other with a kind of visual language, signing their timeless sharing of the light and the day and the light giver that gives light to each of them. The sun has disappeared long since into the darkened west; the sky and the lake remember.

LATE SUMMER

A Hot-Weather Slowdown

NATIVE AMERICANS ONCE CONSTRUCTED SWEAT LODGES to drive away illness and ill spirits; a cleansing for a vision quest, a readying for a challenge. These sultry summer nights redd me only for fall. Lush and damp and noisy with the interwoven voices of a thousand insects, it stays hot until daybreak.

The dawn chorus of birds has changed from spring's frantic territorial competition. Now the birds seem to give voice as if to hear themselves talk, to let the world know they are still here, still kicking. Their fence lines may not be as fiercely claimed and defended, but they stand, nonetheless.

Moths batter against our porch lights and fly in our faces as we come and go. They halo the streetlights like smoke rings and navigate in dizzy circles, mistaking the light for the moon. Bats chitter through the air after them as if on a taut line, darting this way and that, writing an edgy calligraphy on the night sky.

At night the spiders rebuild their webs in every corner and across every path in the woods, so that when I take a dawn walk I trail streamers of spider silk from cheeks and hair and fingers like gossamer ribbons from an arachnid Maypole. Insects use these paths of least resistance, as I do, as do the mammals and birds of the woods. Spiders know that with a predator's instinctive knowing and build their webs where they count. We may find fifty small insects trapped there by morning.

These spiders spin webs from their own body protein each night, to catch as catch can. I wish I were as self-sufficient, as self-contained, as direct. I watch as a garden spider throws out her guy wires and uses them to anchor her perfect orb. She moves with efficiency and accuracy, lifting each line while dipping her spinneret just so to meet it. In less than an hour she is ready for the hunt.

The scents of a late summer night are sweet and evocative. I sink into them as into a cool, northern lake. To tread on bergamot or gill-over-the-ground in the darkness is to be instantly enveloped in spicy sweetness. The heady smell of ozone from a nearby lightning strike is almost tangible on a hot summer night; the Thunder Moon earns its name. The odd fungal smell of mushrooms shouldering up through the soil prickles in our nostrils, unmistakable and indescribable. We sniff like bears.

When drought comes, it chokes the life from summer nights. In a kind of inverted winter dormancy, plants stop their growth and stand panting in the heat. They cannot grow without water. They roll their leaves against moisture loss and pray for a change in the weather. Trapped in the dry earth, the fungal fruiting of mycelium waits for rain. The earth cracks beneath our feet; earthworms dry to leather in their burrows or dig deeper to an eternally moist, root-level night. The earth smells dry, dry as death, and as dusty.

There is still some moisture to be had; Midwestern humidity has its purpose. At night the cool settles in the valleys, flowing downward as if in retreat. Streams exhale in relief into the atmosphere, and a pale blue haze paints the far hills by morning: ground fog. Plants absorb moisture through their leaves; it may be all they get. Humidity, no friend to humans who feel the need of gills on a sultry summer evening, still finds its work in the web of life. For endless August weeks, this blue haze may be the *only* moisture.

And these small bits are enough. Enough to keep night-blooming plants flowering and their insect pollinators fed on schedule. Evening-flowering *Lychnis*, a relative of campion; sweet-scented *Nicotiana* and *Datura*, hanging inverted like huge white ant-lion traps in midair; the primroses and honeysuckles that scented the mellower nights of June and July. These and more float sweet and inviting in the dark. Their scent is overpowering in the pervasive humidity, not light and fresh as in drought.

We wonder if it will ever rain; and when it does, finally, we pay with a mugginess that hangs like a damp shirt. It is late summer in the Midwest, and there is almost too much of it to bear.

JULY 24 • *Early*

The sky is washed with clear, transparent light. The land is still deep in shadow. Pink-touched clouds crowd the blue, as thick as young trees at the edge of a meadow on its way to becoming forest. All along the wooded ridge of Siloam Mountain to the south an echoing forest of clouds wait—for a breeze to push them one way or another. But instead, the small friendly shapes—so close they look touchable over the trees—dissipate in minutes. It is a time-lapse photography study of clouds; they are there, then smaller and smaller until they disappear to blue nothing. Their vapor disperses in the warming air. They were night clouds, nothing more. If I had arrived on my porch ten minutes later I would have missed the show altogether.

I snatch these small moments when I can. Who knows when I would see a sky full of pink puffs like a fantasy of sunrise sheep? Now, twenty minutes later, the sky is as empty as a vacant stare. The clouds have melted in the heat of a rising July sun.

JULY 25 • *Predawn*

A neighbor's barking dog wakes me to the fresh, cool, predawn light. I am groggy with lack of sleep, but this may be the best of this particular day. Weathermen are calling for a hundred degrees and humid by afternoon. I stay up, glad of the chance to feel the morning.

The crows over on Siloam Mountain seem to have been wakened by the dog's barking, as well. I hear them chatting back and forth, calling to each other from tree to tree. From this distance their voices are soft and evocative. I admit to an inordinate fondness for these intelligent big black birds. Cautious as a grandmother on roller skates, they never let me get close enough to really draw them. Quick sketches have to suffice, but even these seem to catch an essential crowness—they are personality kids.

I remember the soft conversations of crows in early morning and evening when I was young. My father took me with him to the hills of the Missouri Ozarks, and the crows would comment on our canoe's passage down the icy, spring-fed streams. They seemed to mock my attempts at learning to paddle. Later in the day they were raucous, noisy, derisive. But early on and late in the evening, there was this softness.

The robins are reclaiming the day as well. All over town, as far as I can hear, territories are announced with a homeowner's pride as they proclaim their audible fence lines.

A mockingbird tunes up sleepily in the tree beside me. He sings only a bit of his variety act before apparently deciding it is too early after all.

I can hear the jays joining in the soft cacophony of dawn. Their voices sound scratchy, out of practice, too long unused—like mine.

On my neighbor's roof ridge the gentle conversations of waking pigeons are mellow, quiet, like the first exchange of the morning between Harris and me. It is as if we want to gentle the act of waking with our voices.

The first of the chimney swifts have risen from their sooty vertical condos and flit just overhead, gleaning prey from the first layer of air just over the houses. Perhaps they are still too tired to fly high—but more than likely these lower air corridors are richest with flying insects at this time of day. As a squadron of them performs a perfect flyby, they chitter rapidly in unison, then steam away beyond my line of vision. By afternoon they will be barely visible pepper grains high overhead, sweeping the cooler layers of air for protein.

JULY 27 • *Evening*

The ancient, leaning fishing pier that pokes like an arthritic finger into Watkins Mill Lake is covered with golden mayflies, newly hatched from naiads in the still, silty water. They are pale lemon-saffron color, lovely

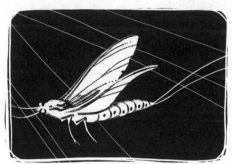

and transitory. They've emerged into the evening light as subimagos; within twenty-four hours they become adult—a very short adolescence, indeed.

This adult form doesn't feed; its only activities are flight and breeding and egg-laying—or falling prey to a hungry fish or low-flying bank swallows. But the naiads that hatch from their eggs feed on the lake bottom a full twelve months before becoming next summer's ephemeral mayflies.

JULY 28 • *Early*

The fisherman creates his own world, carving it out of the night with a lantern. He has brought a lounge chair and a cooler, and he sits on the long gravel spit in the lake, intent on catfish.

Night sounds surround him, soft in the darkness. The long waves race the length of the lake to lap against his light. Off down the cove he hears a sharp slap; a beaver has issued a warning with a broad, flat tail—but a warning against what? Nothing the fisherman needs to fear.

He sees the deer move along the far shore. They came for an early morning drink. Their normal watering holes in the little feeder creek have dried up in the unending heat, one by one. The lake must taste fresh and cool to the big animals; they drink long and slow. They raise their heads at last to stare at the island of light across the lake and at the man contained in its bubble. They have seen these early fishermen before. There is no sense of alarm. Their eyes take in the scene without judgment, like a Zen master.

JULY 29 • *Early morning*

A mosquito, engrossed in dining on my wrist, rode me back inside last night after I fed the cats. I did not even know it was there; it is dark at 11 P.M. and I do not bother taking a flashlight to my familiar porch.

The night was noisy with katydids and crickets. I did not hear the high-pitched whine of the mosquito's wingbeats. The buzz, so loud in the silence of the bedroom, is caused by the speed of those beats—up to one thousand times per second. It is enough to make a hummingbird's eighty beats a second seem like slow motion.

When I got back to the light of the kitchen I noticed my passenger, fat with my blood and still sucking. I slapped it, then studied its engorged abdomen, delicate wings, and spidery, finely haired legs with my pocket microscope.

Within seconds the area of the bite was swollen and itching. I could see the tiny crater where the female mosquito had inserted her tubelike proboscis and six tiny stylets. She needs the protein in my blood to make her eggs—one of the few species of mosquito that do. Most eat fruit and green plants, flying in the face of our prejudice.

To keep the blood flowing freely, she injects an anticoagulant, which makes me itch like fire. Like most of us, I am allergic to her injection.

By this morning the swelling is gone, along with the itch, but the small crater is still in evidence. The anticoagulating chemical also destroys minute amounts of tissue. I will never miss it.

JULY 30 • *Evening*

The gritty, lichen-encrusted concrete of the bridge is still hot against my forearms; it has collected the day's heat and holds it fast. A sickle moon hangs low in the west. I can see its dark side like a shadow through my night glasses. It chases the sun nervously around the earth's curvature as if afraid to be alone this sultry summer night. When it goes there will be only the flickering starlight to see by. The land is dark, nearly black, and spread out beneath the sky. The sky is still the color of my favorite pair of ancient blue jeans.

Silhouetted against its light I see the erratic shapes of bats winnowing the air for insects. And of these there are plenty. I can see clouds of moths near streetlights. They navigate disastrously into the man-made brightness. Gnats and leafhoppers investigate my alien presence on the old half-moon bridge. Hungry mosquitoes have already found my bare arms. I am surprised. Mosquitoes seek heat, and surely there is not much of a differential between my warm flesh and the hot night air. Is it the carbon-dioxide trail they follow tonight?

The bats flutter and turn like paper blown in the wind, yet the seeming randomness is deceiving. They follow the insects' evasive action with unerring skill. In the luminous sky they can still find their prey by sight, but soon their unique method of echolocation using ultrasonic sound will be the best tool. They can discern distance, speed, direction, size, shape, and even surface characteristics with this tool. The bats' method of hunting will stand them in good stead in full dark. For now, they hunt by sight alone. Bats are not, in fact, "blind as a bat"; their sight is quite good. Echolocation is better.

Some moths have developed an ability to hear the high-pitched squeaks of the bat's ultrasonic repertoire. They dodge to escape. No wonder the bats seem to go in all directions at once.

These are most likely little brown bats, *Myotis lucifugus*, common in my part of Missouri. Their Latin name means "mouse-eared light flee-er," an apt enough description of the physical appearance and the nocturnal habits of the tiny mammals. If one can get over a certain prejudice, they are quite handsome creatures with soft fur and somewhat kittenish faces. At just over three inches long, they are nowhere near as threatening as imagination colors them. But then, nothing ever is.

Desultory frogs punctuate the buzz and hum of insects with occasional soprano songs. Perhaps it is too warm even for them. It was over a hundred degrees only two hours ago.

The moon's reflection is a sickly smudge in the scum that covers the big pool under the bridge, but by its wan light I can see slow ripples that tell me something is active in the still water below.

A strange night bird's cry breaks the noisy stillness. I wish I knew its voice. The night still has its secrets, even from an insomniac naturalist.

It is full dark, and at last a cooling breeze moves the leaves. My binoculars are now useless. I cannot even see the antic shapes of bats against the sky. The mosquitoes still land with as much gusto as ever on my arms and hands and neck, the moths fly near the streetlights, and a lingering firefly or two dances over the water. The bats still hunt this rich insect veldt, but invisibly, by sound alone.

JULY 31 • *Early*

A thin morning mist rises off the motionless pool like steam from morning coffee. I brought a portable breakfast to the creek—a bit of sourdough bread, a fresh, cool pear, and a tiny, two-cup flask of coffee. I am waking up slowly, by the riffle.

The big rugged weeds by the path were soaked with the night's heavy dew and with condensation from the creek. The dew gathers in big droplets and runs languidly down a leaf to fall at the tip like rain. Where weeds overhang the path, the fine dust is dotted with moisture; it smells of summer rain after a long drought.

Far off in the old-growth forest I hear the barred owl just returning from the night's hunt. The sun is not yet over the trees upstream, and the air is night cool and refreshing.

An unmusical *scronk* alerts me to the night heron's presence. He, too, must be heading to a quiet perch to rest for the day. Black-crowned night

herons are not so communal as others of their clan. If this one does buddy up, he will keep a private corner for himself. His displaying and mating season is past—the only activities this nocturnal bird pursues in the daylight hours—so if I am lucky I may come upon him later resting by the stream.

His hunting should have been successful here on the Fishing River. This small feeder creek empties into the Missouri.

Along the base of the big clay bank on the north, a hundred crayfish holes tell of a good year for both the little night-active crustaceans and their nemesis, the night heron.

He is elegant, streamlined, and natty in his gray and black plumage. I wish I could have watched that stealthy hunt, the lightning strike of the strong scissors beak. As in the case of all herons, this one does not generally stab a fish or crayfish on that imposing dagger of a bill like shish kebab. Instead, he will most often grab the prey with a quick feint, toss it into the air, and catch it, neat. Herons do skewer an occasional fish, however, then they pull it loose with a foot and reposition their prey for eating.

A kingfisher is up and about. He loops upstream past me, swooping and dipping in his characteristic flight. I see him dive and there is a spray of droplets from his impact, a silver fountain of light. It is morning.

JULY 31 · *Night*

The darkening water slides silently under our canoe, like stealth. In the dusk, cooling a little at last after the day's clanging heat, the lake is the color of burnished pewter.

A canoe's silent passing stirs an atavistic appreciation for the small, graceful craft. It is so perfect. It is so finely designed to its task. It fits me like an old chambray shirt, like an extension of myself. I think turn, and we turn. I think stop, and we stop. I think glide, or speed up, or float soundlessly toward the shore, and we do just that.

My husband and I work together to maneuver the silver shaft of the canoe, as we have for twenty-three years—smoothly, but with a certain syncopated rhythm. The years have not quite made us one. But the canoe moves forward like the very idea of motion itself, effortlessly slipping through the evening.

It is an uneventful paddle on the still lake. I see—or think I see—an immense frog suspended in the water, its back to us, looking toward the shore. It is a weathered and waterlogged limb. I imagine the shape of a deer standing among the oaks on shore. It is a shadow. I strain my eyes to find a great blue heron's upright form among the broken trees, but if he is there he is as motionless as they and has like as not returned to the heronry at this time of night. Only the pale flash of a common tern moves through the evening like a white moth, like a silver canoe, a light streak smudged into the night. The still, elegant paddling is itself an event, broken only by the musical fall of droplets from our paddles.

The night is the perfect anniversary gift to ourselves. Quiet and cool and as good together as ever.

AUGUST 1 · Night

A ride through a Midwestern country midnight takes us through pools of scent so intense as to be tangible. Why can't I *see* those invisible veils that brush my face with their aromas? Why don't my headlights find a rich green drying to cellophane gold as I pass through the evocative scent of drying hay on the night air? Why don't I see an amber-brown haze when I drive over an invisible creek bed in the darkness?

Instead, two weeks into a drought with daytime temperatures reaching a hundred and five degrees, the backcountry road is a colorless ghost in my headlights, a tunnel powdered with limestone gravel dust. In the rearview mirror I see a pale wraith kicked up by my tires, thick as fog. It rises to treetop level and falls on the unresisting leaves; they hang still and accepting in the airless night. Another layer is added to thick coating on the leaves, delineating them against the darkness like a scratchboard drawing in ink.

AUGUST 3 · *Early Sunday morning*

I hoped to make it up in time to watch the chimney swifts pour from the big smokestack on Marietta Street, but they are up long before the sun and chittering madly through the air.

It should not surprise me that they are early risers. These birds are the workaholics of the avian world. They are up past dark in their diligent attempt to clear the small-town skies of insect life. As still another hungry mosquito finds my warmth, I cheer them on.

These type-A birds never even take a coffee break. Their small, weak feet are no good for perching, anyway. They cling best to vertical surfaces, propped by their tails. The abrupt uprights of chimneys and smokestacks and such suit them best. The baby birds begin their practice early, perching outside their mud and saliva nests as if they cannot wait to join the rat race.

Soon enough they will join their elders for those dawn-to-dusk raids on the airways, darting and fluttering, gliding high overhead or almost close enough to touch, singly or in chattering groups.

In a walk to the nearby woods I discover an orb weaver spider. She has spent a profitable night. Her web is a harvest festival of small, night-flying insects. I count twenty-two midges, moths, and mosquitoes, including the one she is dismembering as I watch. Her web is torn from the night's activity on the busy path, but she can take her leisurely pick of prey—appetizers, entrées, and desserts.

As I watch she twirls the remains in silk for later, as tidy as a housewife with a roll of plastic wrap. She manages to brace herself, turn the prey insect around and around with her feet, and spin a fine cord with her spinneret to wrap it in, all at the same time. Obviously she needs all eight legs.

AUGUST 4 · *Evening into night*

The long heat wave is finally broken, and the evening cool is as welcome as world peace. The temperature dropped ten degrees in an hour as clouds slid overhead, pulling a billowy awning over us to protect us, at last, from the sun. Ninety degrees feels suddenly pleasant, bearable.

It is too lovely to waste. We drive into the country, not caring if the sparking black clouds open up, not caring if all we do is drive into the storm encased in our steel envelope, not caring if we get—at last—good and wet.

Watkins Mill Lake is our destination. I want to see these lovely, varying clouds reflected in that broad mirror. And if there is a break in the clouds, sunset will be spectacular. Already the west sends hints: the golden eye of the sun peers through a hole in the clouds, assessing the situation.

The light is lovely, poignant. The clouds shimmer mother-of-pearl, iridescent shades of gray and peach and lavender. Against the unbroken gunmetal of the east, this strange light throws the land into sharp relief, oddly lighter now than the sky—glowing, pale green. Each smallest detail is painfully, touchingly sharp, as if seen after a long absence. I feel a homecoming as if I woke after a long coma to the sweet, green hills of Missouri.

We drive through the wooded campground in the strange and lovely light. Under the trees, each campsite is dark and shadowed like the mouth of a cave, inviting as a home den after a long hunt. Where the road tunnels light between the oaks, each leaf is distinct and clean as if seen through the finest photographic lens. It is an Ansel Adams light—evocative, beautiful. We stand and gawk like tourists.

Just beyond the campground the land opens itself to the sky, not a narrow tunnel of sky between the trees, but a big sky, a prairie sky, one that reaches to forever and beyond. I feel myself open up as well and expand. The sky is a magnet. Where else *could* I look tonight? As if to add the final touch of perfection, the dying sun reaches across the lake to catch a shower of rain. The broad arc of a rainbow bridges the wooded camp we just left.

The lake itself is nearly deserted. Mecca to hundreds of the overheated in recent weeks, now the delicious cool is shared by only one other party. As we approach the shore, fishermen launch their johnboat to cast away the night. Fish are biting in the sudden cool. I see their silver rings and hear the soft liquid plop as they leap after an abundant hatch of August mayflies. It will be a good night for fishing.

I am fishing only for the night itself. We lie back on the cool planks of the old dock to watch the changeling sky and to wait for full dark. The weather is unstable; there is a manic excitement in the air.

Layers of clouds pass overhead, each moving at its chosen speed, each wearing its own shade of evening. In the west the far clouds are salmon

and peach; overlaying these are blue-gray ribbons that tie the hemispheres together. The east is dark. Paynes' gray clouds mutter with lightning and reach long pale fingers of electricity across the miles. I smell the sharp ozone of the light. Overhead, a high, chill cloud is struck by an errant beam of sunset light. It is pale against the darkening skies above it.

Our imaginations soar with the clouds: here is a featherbed, there Shiva and a snake, and in the south, a river delta suspended in midair. Once I thought a tornado reached toward earth and then disappeared, sucked back into the mother cloud.

We watched until full dark. The coolness was bone deep, caressing my bare arms like silk, running sweet, cool fingers through my hair. A whippoorwill, tuning up on the far bank, raised an answer down the darkened lake and then fell silent.

AUGUST 6 · *10:30 P.M.*

Something skittered away across the backyard when I stepped out to feed our ancient cat. I heard it race through the garden, rattling the leaves deadened prematurely by the population explosion of oak lace bugs.

It may have been the raccoon; he is very shy of me, still, and often visits the cat food cans after dark. Last night I heard him around midnight, snuffling and clanking among the empties.

He is after the dry cat food as well. He is not choosy, food is food. He softens it in the cats' water dish, picking up each tiny donut shape with his sensitive front feet and dunking it in a parody of a coffee-shop breakfast. It is to soften the food as well as to sensitize his handlike paws to touch that he most likely performs this ritual, not to fastidiously wash as I was told as a child. How surprised he must be when his "donuts" dissolve in the water! Each morning I find a grainy residue at the bottom of the dish and have to wash the container again. He must be far too thorough in his dunkings. It takes a while to dissolve dry cat food. *Procyon lotor* is named for this odd habit. *Lotor* means "one who washes."

AUGUST 7 • 3:00 A.M.

The barred owls have left their territorial preserves in East Valley Park and branched out for the hunt. They hunt together tonight; I can hear their voices calling out to one another, triangulating the hill into manageable portions. They are just outside my bedroom window, or rather the big male is. I hear his mate over on the hill, returning her own news about luck and hunting conditions and the availability of prey.

They identify each other by voice. They recognize a friendly inflection in the dark. Perhaps a certain lilt in the female's hoot that tells the male there is no need to ride to the defense of his territory. This owl call, at least, is friend rather than foe. *Hoo hoo hoo-hoo, hoo hoo hoo hoooo-aw-w-w-w*—a familiar voice in the darkness.

I was sleeping like a stone when they started up just outside. It is a fitting revenge for the times I have wakened them in the daytime with my owl call tapes. I wonder if they heard the taped calls in my quadrant of their territory and think the sound must mean the hunting is good here, good enough to support a rival. I have not used the tape in a few weeks. Perhaps they assume the poacher is long gone, and there will be abundant small gray furry things to eat and no competition for them at all.

This pair seems to be making good and certain any lingering interloper knows they are here. They make a fearsome racket. If I were another owl, I would certainly hesitate to intrude on territory defended so vocally by these two; they sound like twenty. Their calls are loud and fierce. The sounds interweave and overlap, coming one on top of another so quickly I can hardly sort them out. "A variety of . . . barking calls and screams," according to the *Audubon Field Guide*. I'll say.

AUGUST 8 • 9:45 P.M.

It has been so dry this summer that there are no nocturnal slugs skating slowly through the garden, no slime trails on the back screen, no competition at the cats' bowl, except for mammal scavengers.

Last year I stepped out on the porch in my bare feet and squashed one underfoot—a most unpleasant experience, and one that evokes a heartfelt "yeec-c-c-ch!" It took forever to wash the mucilaginous slime from the sole of my foot. It was like partially dried and particularly tenacious glue. I have removed epoxy more easily.

Tonight I take my flashlight to the rock garden to check for signs of slug life. Lifting heavy rocks, I expect to find slugs and bugs and all manner of life in the moist earth, but I find only dry, crumbled tunnels and two light-shy pill bugs. The drought is serious when I miss slugs and their silvery trails of slime.

They are protected by this thick, slimy coating, but not in extremes of drought. It is not waterproof, and slugs and their close cousins, the snails, dry out rapidly through evaporation. Though they are mainly nocturnal, I may still see them about in the woods after a rain.

It is their highly developed sense of smell that leads them to the cats' pan. A slug can smell food from more than half a meter away and adjust his course accordingly.

AUGUST 9 • *Predawn*

The smoke alarm's intermittent bleat drags me from my bed at 4:45 A.M. I do not know how long it has been demanding my attention. The raucous, insistent sound was tangled in my dreams, and I had managed to explain it away in some implausible scenario.

I can smell no smoke, after a quick check indoors and out, and the syncopated shriek seems all wrong. I call the fire department anyway. They tell me a spider or a bit of dust probably set it off, since it was an irregular, pulsing shriek and not a sustained repetition. When I move it to another place it stops. Guess they were right, but my adrenalin level does not buy it. I am up for the day.

I step outside to midnight darkness; dawn drags its feet these days, and the sky is as black and starry as midnight. They sparkle like a childhood dream of enough—finally enough—stars to wish upon.

It is early for the Perseid meteor showers, but as I watch, the sky lights up with a quick, lovely streak heading south. A few moments later, another zips off north by northeast. All this activity sends me hotfooting back indoors for my calendar of natural events put out by the Missouri Department of Conservation. I was right; those dawn walkers were not due for another four or five days.

But in any case, orphan bits of comets rain down on us like a summer shower any night of the year. Most are so small they burn out invisibly in the upper atmosphere. The larger ones, made up of ice and iron and rock, flare like a lit match in the darkness at the rate of twenty per hour. I probably just happened upon a one-two punch to the stratosphere.

This dawn is a silent one, except for the songs of tree crickets and katydids overhead and the rasp of a field cricket by the porch. No dawn chorus of birds, even by 5:30 A.M. But then, dawn still seems a long way off in this transparent darkness.

A warm smudge in the east advertises coming attractions; one small wisp of cloud is mauve with reflected daybreak.

The meteors may be ahead of schedule; the day started early—too early—but the dawn chorus of birds is late. A male cardinal finally breaks the silence. Within minutes the resident robins stir, adding tentative first notes to his. A nightjar is busy sweeping the mosquito-laden air; I hear his distinctive *boom*.

By 6:15 A.M. the sky has faded to the same pale blue as my favorite chambray work shirt. The stars have leached out of the morning sky entirely. The rush-hour traffic of chimney swifts has begun, all going west to east. Can they all live in the smokestack condo downtown? With their coming, morning is officially here, sunrise or no.

That event is slated for 6:24 A.M., according to my almanac. But it is a no-show. An impromptu sun-searching drive to the eastern rim of hills in my nightgown makes me reflect ruefully on one of my husband's most astute observations: naturalists do weird things. This makes my mother's admonition never to leave the house in torn underwear pale in comparison.

But at least I find the sun; it is hung up in a low bank of clouds, invisible from our valley. The clouds are all that remain of our promise of rain.

AUGUST 9 · *Night*

A trip to a gallery opening offered the rare chance to observe a big-city night. The tall buildings and millions of square feet of concrete act as a giant solar collector, trapping the heat of the day long after dark and radiating it back like a memory of anger. The sidewalks were solidified steam. Noises magnified in the heat until it felt like fever.

The moon radiated heat as well—big and hot and golden, brooding low and sullen over the buildings. It was the hottest night of the year, the night of the full moon. On nights like this, crime in the city is multiplied by double. We go crazy in the unending heat and glare. There is no relief in darkness. Heat rolls off the people and buildings, streets and sidewalks. Tempers blaze hot as sun glare.

But still, the air is full of nightjars as it is in my small town. A huge owl flies in silhouette against the television tower. The moonlight reflects in the hot black asphalt as in the smooth surface of a lake.

AUGUST 10 · *10:30 P.M.*

A loud, measured ticking arouses my curiosity and draws me to the front porch, flashlight in hand. Has someone planted a bomb on the doorstep?

It is a big male fork-tailed bush katydid, almost three inches long. At first the sound seems to come from everywhere, but as I step off the porch I realize I must have walked right under the noisy serenader. I finally find it by pulling down a mulberry limb.

The insect is nearly the same shade as the glossy leaves and shaped like folded leaves as well. But those beadlike red eyes and long legs and swivelling sensitive antennae give him away. The red eyes and forked sex organs mark him as a male.

He finally tires of my constant pulling his perch this way and that to get a better look. It must be like riding a bull. He flies away to a more private, steady, and inaccessible branch to continue his drumbeat. I can see him just out of my reach, testing and tasting his new perch with his long antennae. They are covered with fine, hairlike sensors, and he is making sure the new place is to his liking—and safe from predators and inquisitive naturalists.

AUGUST 11 · *Early hours*

The alarm I have set for 2:30 A.M. rouses me from a deep sleep to instant realization: I want to see the Perseid meteor shower tonight, and there is no better time to do it than these small, dark hours.

But tonight the moon is too near full and slow in passing through. It drowns the night sky in a melting light, obscuring everything but the brightest and boldest of stars. It hangs in the southern hemisphere, still nearly overhead, as if reluctant to relinquish territory. A veil of mackerel clouds helps to obscure the meteor showers.

An invisible jet splits the small-hour silence. If I cannot see its lights through the opaque haze there is not much chance of catching a shower of space dust as it rains through earth's upper atmosphere.

The clouds take on fantastic shapes in the moonlight—sinister, reaching. They drag across the sky like raking fingers or are pulled into many-legged octopi with stars in their greedy tentacles. It is light enough to write without my flashlight. My hand throws a moon shadow on the page, so insistent is the pale silver glow.

Still, it is lovely to be up. Snowy tree crickets hold a long, sustained note in the trees around me, a note that pulsates slightly as first one insect and then another takes up the refrain. Insomniac katydids punctuate this one-note serenade with their repetitious *katydi-i-i-d, katy-di-i-i-i-id* in a blizzard of commas and periods.

A noise of chewing tells me that the nocturnal raccoon is into the cat food. I am so silent, so still here that he has overlooked my presence entirely and feasts on the last of the food. He always leaves the bowl empty, no matter how much food I have put out. The freeloader deserves his bandit's mask.

I use my father's night glasses to scan the sky, leaning back in the old-fashioned metal lawn chair. These glasses find a few more stars than my naked eye in the milky darkness, and finally—by sheer luck—a few streaks of meteor. But the glasses are heavy at 2:30 A.M., and the metal chair makes my bones ache. I yawn once, then twice, then give up the vigil. I will catch the next show in October, when the Orionids meteor shower is set to begin, unless it, too, is no-show, drowned in moonlight.

AUGUST 13 • *Early*

H. A. Dickey tells me of a magical predawn sight encountered on his morning walk around Watkins Mill Lake. Four young deer, still gangly but old enough to begin to lose their spots, played tag with each other around a fat pine tree, chasing around and around the tree. Nearby, a doe stood watch, grazing peacefully but alert to any danger.

Deer normally have twins and occasionally only one. Quadruplets are rare indeed. Was this doe the appointed guardian for the day, a deer's equivalent of a baby sitter? Wolves behave in this way, leaving an older sibling or an aunt or uncle with the youngsters while parents leave for the hunt. Perhaps the doe watched someone else's fawns as well as her own. And like all young animals, these practiced at real life in their play, ducking and running and dodging around the tree. Their quicksilver agility will come in handy later.

AUGUST 14 • *Predawn*

A few anxious songbirds have already begun their long migration. In the daytime I hear a stranger singing in my trees, a lovely voice normally heard only in deep woods. No expert birder, I can only guess at a hermit thrush's lilting, exotic song. At night—or at least at this predawn hour—there is a nearly constant chatter overhead in the darkness, a moving blanket of sound heading southward. It is early for the main migrations by nearly a month. I wonder what flies invisibly in the dark, talking softly overhead? There is a low ceiling of nimbostratus clouds threatening rain and deadening all sound but this "conversation." The birds fly below it for better visibility.

Perhaps they talk to one another companionably on the long journey—as we do—to break the monotony, to keep spirits up, to keep ourselves awake.

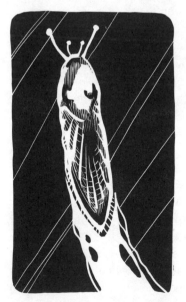

AUGUST 15 • *Night*

The welcome rain brought somewhat less welcome grass growth. Harris had to mow this morning. But after dark when I went out barefoot to walk in it, it was heavenly, like the deepest of cool, green moss.

And finally, when I went out on the back porch at midnight—slugs in the cat pan. The long slug-free drought is over. They had not been able to move on their self-lubricated slime trails over that gritty, dry earth, I suppose. Who would have thought I would miss slugs?

AUGUST 16 · *Night*

A harvestman tickles my forearm as he walks, as bold as brass, across my bare skin, as if I were only another part of the landscape. His long legs are light, whispery, four to a side and as long as a katydid's antennae. And in fact, the second and longer pair of legs is used in this way—to feel, to sense, to test.

This common daddy longlegs was on his way to a town meeting of the delicate-legged creatures. Just beyond the abandoned garden a group of some fifteen to twenty adults stand, legs tangled together and waving. What must they communicate in this way?

I do not bother them. Their best defense is a nasty stench, released when they are pressed. And they need a defense. If they lose one of those delicate, feelerlike legs they are unable to grow a new one.

AUGUST 17 · *Night*

An insect song—so loud—called me from the front of the house to the back garden. My curiosity must be assuaged! I took the flashlight out to discover the singer and to catch him in the act. When I stepped outside the sound was nearly deafening—high and strident and loud.

This loudest of katydids—the Nebraska conehead—was in the garden among my tomatoes. After climbing through the strongly scented vines and dew-wet weeds, I found him clinging upside down to a tomato leaf.

Even the beam of my light did not stop his singing. His wings were held in a rigid double bow, stridulating madly against each other—up to forty times a second to make that high whine.

AUGUST 18 · *5:15 P.M.*

A false dusk settled early tonight and with it the tornado sirens and hailstones. The sky, minutes before, had billowed with angry greenish clouds like painful swellings against a black background—the kind of clouds you know are full of wind.

They were. In Mosby, the small town down the road, the roof was lifted from a lumber company and scattered over the countryside, and hundred-year-old trees were turned to matchsticks. At nearby Smithville Lake, RVs were flipped on their sides like dying dinosaurs; boats were overturned and swamped; docks were ripped loose from their moorings and set afloat like lost houseboats.

Weather experts say they were straight-line winds, but the waitress at our local café (who lives in Mosby) says she saw a tail dragging from the wall of black clouds as the roof was ripped away.

By 6:00 P.M. the storm had passed, and the sky was light again, with openings in the clouds big enough to put a heartland county in.

Later I glanced out of a southern window to see a gorgeous bank of wind-filled clouds lit to an eerie melon color by the setting sun. A pinch of that sight through the kitchen window was not anywhere near enough. We hopped in the car and drove to the airport on the hill to see the whole unbelievable sky arching overhead from horizon to horizon.

The unstable weather with its opposing fronts was spread out like a textbook visual aid to meteorology. The vast field of tornado-breeding mammatocumulus clouds, on fire with the setting of the sun, filled a third of the sky. To the west, a new storm was building. Tall mountainous cumulus clouds wore Maxfield Parrish linings of hot orange light. We could see the long streaks of peach and salmon reaching out from behind them. As the sun slid farther behind the cloud bank, we could see the light streaks being pulled across the field of wind-puffed clouds as if someone had painted them in bold, alternating strokes—salmon, gray, salmon, gray.

In the north, a thunderstorm was in progress. Flashes of lightning reached from black clouds to the ground below, bathing everything momentarily in white glare. The rain fell like thick, dark draperies a few miles away, ringing down the curtain on the hills beyond. But above and beyond these violent black clouds, a single, beautiful cumulus cloud caught the light of the setting sun, glowing as if from a compliment. It was a spectacular sky, a meteorologist's dream.

AUGUST 20 • *Night*

Nearly tangible on the night air, the scent of skunk rises up from the road and slaps me across the face, still belligerent.

It is that pugnaciousness that did in the nocturnal skunk in the first place, pugnaciousness and a certain surety in his own most excellent line of defense. How was the skunk to know that the glowing eyes of someone's headlights were two tons of steel and immune to the threat of olfactory mayhem?

It happens all the time; skunk stands his ground, drumming defiance with his tiny feet, then lifts that brush of a tail in a defensive arc—and splat!

AUGUST 23 • *Night*

Peering under boards and rocks in the garden, I found a ubiquitous common ground beetle searching for worms and small caterpillars. Shiny as black patent leather, this beetle is found coast to coast—you almost cannot fail to find him scouting about for prey.

Best he hunt with one eye out for the hunter. He, too, is common prey for the tiny shrews in these parts.

My neighbor found a shrew that had a run-in with a cat and brought it to me for identification. The soft, gray-brown fur; long nose; tiny eyes; large, hidden ears; and stubby tail made it unmistakably a short-tailed shrew—that and its size, only three and three-quarters inches from nose tip to tail.

These voracious little creatures have a bigger appetite than I do, and it keeps them hopping. A shrew will eat from three-quarters to more than its own body weight a day, just to keep up its constant nervous activity. Its metabolism is on permanent fast forward. A shrew is not thought of as nocturnal, *per se*, but with that kind of need for food calories, it takes day and night feeding to keep it going.

AUGUST 25 • *Night*

The limestone rocks in the forest are covered with wood lice of all sizes that crawl about in a businesslike fashion. These little gray armadillos help break down the damp leaves and bits of rotting wood to make new soil. Like the slug, they have no protective covering to keep them safe from the drying rays of the sun. They love the night.

I touch one with the tip of my pencil. It rolls up tightly in a ball. No wonder we called them roly-poly bugs when I was a kid.

AUGUST 26 • *Evening*

A blind-eyed sphinx moth tries to startle me by revealing the bright "eyes" of its underwings. It is a perfect example of protective adaptation. If I had been a predatory bird or a shrew, intent on a fat moth for a bedtime snack, those huge eyes appearing from nowhere would shock me right out of my carnivorous notions. They have a threatening scowl with glowering pink lids to match the horrid fat body. It is an excellent disguise.

When his upper wings are "shut," he is almost perfectly camouflaged against the tree bark, an additional defense that works well for him. He is one of the most common Missouri moths.

AUGUST 27 • *Night*

The sound of a train whistle stretches endlessly in the night and touches me with memory and a kind of bone-deep longing. The sound carries for miles. I can hear the train's iron wheels at a crossing, a double clack-*clack*, clack-*clack*, clack-*clack*. The roar and rumble seems a part of me; the train travels along my veins, whistles with my breath.

I grew up between two sets of railroad tracks and picked the tramp flowers that had come to my small corner of Missouri all the way from New York and Montana and Oregon. I carted home tadpoles from the ditches along the tracks and watched them turn into tiny frogs. I listened to the mythic tales of the men who rode the rails and dreamed of doing the same someday. I learned Morse code from my elderly neighbor, long retired from a life with the railroad.

This midnight sound is no stranger to me; it is a part of the land-scape of night. Odd how sounds worn smooth by familiarity become part of the natural world to us, as normal to the night as the call of a nighthawk, the sometime fluttering of a bat, or the cry of a coyote. Citizens of New York, where there is no small-hour silence, must become used to sirens and the honking of horns and shouts in the streets, as acclimated to these sounds as I am to the sounds of trains. I would never have heard this one if it were not for a bit of late-night insomnia.

It is a welcome insomnia with a train whistle in it. The sound takes me to places I have never been, places of my dreams. The long rumble enters my imagination as a question. Where? And why? And why can't I go, too?

AUGUST 28 • *Sunset*

The setting sun throws alternate bars of light and shadow across the curv-ing park road. I rode my ancient bicycle to savor the cool of the evening.

After the steel-mill blaze of July and August, I feel the earth turn its face from the sun with satisfaction, with gratitude. We have stared that relentless, glowing disc in the face long enough. After a summer such as this one, an instant turn into winter would be welcome. Go ahead; crank her a half-turn.

I feel as if I am breaking free of summer, breaking out of jail as I sail past those shadowed bars on fat balloon tires. The cool evening with its rich scents has given me back the joy and abandon of youth. I pedal like crazy just to feel dusk sliding past my face.

AUGUST 30 • *4:30 A.M.*

The only early birds about are on the road, commuting to jobs in the city in the half light. The dawn chorus begins later and later as the daylight shrinks, and the night stretches on either end to take up the slack.

It has been a long summer, full and yeasty, overflowing its normal bounds with its heat. The hint of autumn is welcome. It cannot come too soon.

TATTERS OF SUMMER

We Reclaim the Night

THERE IS PROMISE IN THE AIR, A HINT OF CHANGE. The sultriness of July and August abates. The heat is simply that, and passing.
Nights cool, and there is freshness and repose in these dark hours. A
campfire feels like home instead of torture, and when I cook our dinner
there I no longer put out the fire as soon as possible. I sit and dream and
put off inevitable sleep.

There are promises of new life to be found in the seeding and dying
of summer flowers and in the cocoons and galls that decorate the stems
of weeds and the underside of leaves. Summer's insects have planted
the seeds of life beneath the bark of trees and deep in the earth; cicadas
and snowy tree crickets and katydids have laid plans for the future.

At dusk, mosquitos are still active, and hornets taste and test and
make off with bits of sweetness from a fallen apple they have hollowed
to the skin. Wasps plan for the survival of their queen over winter, making preparations in the early evening of the year.

The earth turns toward equinox, and change is put on fast forward.
From early September's hot nights to late September's cool air, we might
miss the season altogether, asleep like Rumpelstiltskin. There may be
frost when we awake.

Still there are insects in the grass, singing as if the winter would
never come, and even if their voices are lower and slower, their prospec-
tive mates still recognize the message.

Beavers step up their preparations for the cold months, working
through the night to down as many trees as possible. Some of their small
cuttings will strengthen dams or lodges, others will be put by in the
beaver's underwater larder against the time when ice denies access to the
land. In the thin light of a new day, we find that they have nearly cut
through a fine, big elm that leans over the water. They will strip the
branches of this big tree of their tender twigs and insure survival until
the spring.

Mice are active at the harvest. They stock their dens through the
night. Owls may find them there and eat well, no longer sharing with
hungry nestlings. The young are on their own.

The rain in the air smells sweet on the dry earth. In these short weeks of leftover summer, change is everywhere, and summer becomes early autumn.

SEPTEMBER 1 • *Late evening*

Frogs seem to whistle up the night at the lake; it comes to their sweet piping, obedient. The noisy shores are inky and darkening by the minute. A dark watercolor stain spreads downward in the water and runs softly into sky color.

A half-moon and soft clouds are reflected in the still water. In the darkest reflections we see the concentric rings of a school of feeding fish scribed on the surface of the lake. A killdeer skips like a stone over the water and snatches up dinner on the wing, as efficient at fishing as an osprey. Small shiners or the fry of larger fish are the killdeer's prey.

We finished our dinner: garlicky steaks grilled over the campfire, cold beans with bacon. Nothing tastes so good as food cooked over an open fire and seasoned with the smoky hunger of a long day spent outdoors.

The frogs are so noisy I can barely hear the whippoorwill across the lake. He is a bit halfhearted in any case. Territorial concerns have passed, young are raised, and he sings only to himself.

We sit mesmerized by the orange flames of the campfire that slide up over the blackened logs, and we try to read the calligraphy of smoke.

"There's something about a campfire that makes you feel secure," Harris observes, "something primeval."

He is right. It is an aboriginal security, ancient as man's own success at survival—we have fire. We control at least one small part of our lives.

Fire, tools, art—with these we have forged a civilization. We are clearly defined in the mirror of evolution, and we know our own reflection there. Our fire, a perfect admixture of fuel and air and heat, puts us in touch with the dawn of our culture, our own evolving story. The uses we put it to—life-sustaining heat, light, the forging of tools—are timeless.

The green well of trees our tent inhabits has shrunk, now, to the flickering roof of leaves touched by firelight. Its depth varies, the verdant roof moves farther away or closer in as a log catches and flares or disappears to darkening embers.

Far overhead, silver stars are snagged in the branches. Off to the southwest, milk white moonlight stains the sky with opaque light. It reaches through the leaves to touch my face. As I walk in the dark beyond the fire's circle, I feel this light caress my eyelids.

In the tops of the trees, snowy tree crickets sing a song as constant as moonlight. It is a sound of sleigh bells, fat tiny bells marked with an open cross—the kind we heard when we were young. Hounds bay somewhere on the neighboring hills—farm dogs maddened by moonlight and the scent of coon. A great horned owl booms once, twice, and is answered by his mate. Knowing her whereabouts, he clams up as if satisfied. And down on the lake we hear the resident flock of Canada geese coming in for a landing. Their webbed feet kick up the moonlight and send it out around them in waves.

We retire to the tent content to the bone. The warmth of our old double sleeping bag will feel good against the cool of night.

SEPTEMBER 2 • *Early*

We missed the sunrise by twenty minutes or so; campfire and coffee were too appealing by far. We could not move. Now we sit on the old dock, listening to the early morning cries of bloodthirsty killdeer and the *fee-bee* calls of a flock of chickadees and the sharp *chip* of a cardinal. Back at camp, the dawn chorus was differentiated from the robins and titmice and cardinals at home by the varied population of woodpeckers. Flickers, downies, hairies, red-heads, red-breasted—each added his almost mechanical whirr, his rapid drumbeat to our reveille. With that drum and bugle corps, who could sleep?

SEPTEMBER 3 • *Night*

I sit alone by the fire in the singing night, after a day of lovely, long silences. We were comfortable with each other; words were an unnecessary encumbrance, excess baggage.

Now on our last night in the woods I cannot bear to go to bed. I will probably lie there unsleeping. Last night I savored the hours until nearly dawn and did not mind the wakefulness. Coyote song, train whistles, the voice of the great horned owl that seemed to have taken up residence just overhead—It was a good night for not sleeping. There was hickory-nut hail on the tent and the hard earth around us. We could hear them strike and bounce and skitter across the bare ground, an unceasing rain of sound.

Even after the clouds hid the bold half-moon, the tent's thin nylon ceiling glowed with pale light. Even in the deep woods, even at night,

the sky—the light giver— sends measurable brightness. I went out sometime deep in the night. There is no tyrant clock here in camp to tell me how much sleep I am missing, and who cares? I could see where I was going simply by the pale pervasive light that sifted through the trees like unbleached flour.

We saw the owl on the way back to camp tonight.

He was high on top of a dead snag as if to get a clear view of us. But as soon as I stopped to get my binoculars, he was off. He had no desire to be the object of our curiosity. Even at that distance I could see the feathered "ear" tufts that give this largest of the eared owls its name. Even at that distance I could see his wings must have measured upwards of fifty-five inches. It must have been his *hoo, hoo-hoo, HOO HOO* I heard rattle the night.

SEPTEMBER 4 • *Early*

Early bird cormorants dry off after diving by holding their wings out like Dracula's cape. They look like big black Anhingas, misplaced here on a Midwestern lake. They are less waterproof than other waterfowl. They do not have the oil sac that ducks and geese use to keep their feathers drip-dry. This apparent disadvantage is the cormorant's best fishing secret. Such easily waterlogged feathers allow him to sink and dive effectively. Air sacs let him spend as long as a minute or more underwater. We counted the endless seconds as one big bird dove after his prey: seventy-eight.

This summer I watched the cormorant pair pant in the heat to cool off. Their orange throat pouches fluttered like a frog's. Their dark color absorbs heat like a solar collector.

Oddly prehistoric birds, the double-crested cormorants like a wide variety of habitats. We have seen them here for two years. Last year, the lake level was lowered to work on the swimming beach. A small breeding colony of cormorants decorated a dead tree at the water's edge like Christmas ornaments. The exposed freshwater mussel beds attracted a wide variety of bird life. Herons and gulls and terns all vied for the fresh meat. The cormorants took no part in this feast.

SEPTEMBER 4 • *Evening*

A hornet explores me like strange terrain—tastes my salt, cools my flesh with the small breeze of his wings. I am at home with him and with his apparent curiosity. I share that need to explore, to taste, to feel, to know.

I feel his scratchy insect feet on my arm. They move slowly toward my wrist where the skin is thin and transparent. His mandibles touch and lick my skin. If he wanted, he could cause me a jolt. My field guide calls hornets a nuisance to humans. Their sting is painful, or so I am told. I simply share experience with him and with his kind, allow myself to be explored, to be known and, in turn, to know him to be benign unless threatened. I, too, explore and taste and wander. I, too, am dangerous if threatened.

SEPTEMBER 5 • *Night*

Our back door cat was entertaining a visitor when I stepped out to feed him after dark. Old Silver, the big 'possum, was lounging on the patio companionably. The two were like a pair of cats, and old friends, at that.

I broke the spell. Old Silver became quicksilver instead and slid quickly into the hole under the porch. I could see his scaly tail disappear virtually under my feet and heard him scuffling about, making for the basement. I wonder if he will winter there again? I will watch for a buildup of dead leaves next month. Opposums pick them up by the handful, pass them down under their bellies, and stuff as many as possible into that prehensile tail to carry to the den site. One year the basement was a leaf pile of oak and elm and hickory and box-elder; it needed raking.

SEPTEMBER 6 • *Night*

There is a faint ring around the moon, and it is almost full. With the spotty clouds turned pearl gold by the moonlight, it is spectacular.

My grandfather said that a ring around the moon means rain, and

perhaps it is so. According to my weather book, that is one legend that has basis in fact and observation. A ring around the moon *does* mean rain, about 75 percent of the time and within forty-eight hours, if the pressure is falling rapidly.

I am awakened later by the sound of a wreck up the hill. It has sprinkled, and the road is slick. Someone has missed the curve and careened into my neighbor's car.

SEPTEMBER 7 · *Late evening*

I stepped out into the evening to make sure my small cat's grave is still well covered. We buried her last night, a victim of feline leukemia and feline infectious peritonitis—the ground was summer hard, like stone. We should have dug the grave deeper by half again, but I had planned to cover it with something heavy today to protect it from scavengers.

An old galvanized bucket is close at hand; and, since it is getting late, I decide to grab it for a temporary cover. It has stood on the same spot for a month. I disturb a community of small bucket dwellers when I move their safe home. Pill bugs, crickets, a huge spider, and a garter snake scatter in the sudden light.

The snake is a small one. I make a grab to pick it up as it slides away under the log chopping block, but it is strong, amazing so, for its eight-inch length. It tugs—I pull. It tugs harder, I hang on. And then, horrified, I find myself holding only the tip end of the unfortunate snake's tail. It thrashes about blindly, violently, as if looking for its body.

It writhes with life and with a phantom pain I feel in my gut. I drop it as if scalded as the snake makes good his getaway, not stopping to mourn his tail.

I am disgusted with myself. I feel like a bully, one who would pull the wings off flies. I should have known that grabbing that slender bit of snake would end in disaster, for the snake and for my self-esteem as a pacifist naturalist.

But the naturalist's curiosity prevails over my disgust. I pick up the one-inch segment of snake and hold it in my hand. It still whips blindly as if to search for its lost self. How can it be so live, so active? The dot of blood at the end is already drying, sealing the wound.

I watch it, mesmerized, for fully five minutes, and still it moves, attempting to crawl away. It is getting dark. It is time to go in, and I take the snake piece with me. How long will this dim half-life remain?

Half an hour later, it is motionless, even when I touch it. I am awed by the intensity of that urge and by its staying power. It is a different kind of life from our own sentient, thinking being. After fifteen minutes or so it was a simple firing of electrical impulses, but not life in the same way that the snake itself is alive. But that knowledge does not soak in when you watch a one-inch bit of snake turn and wriggle in your hand. It is *life*. Or it was.

And what will become of the snake? It was a harmless ribbon snake, slender as a whippet. I am sickened to have harmed it.

SEPTEMBER 8 · *Midnight*

A day full of too much of everything has the neurons in my brain firing like popcorn. I am on overload—frustration, creativity, tension, anxiety, people, phone calls, missed connections, ideas bucketing through my brain like freight trains. All this has led to a night of insomnia. I sit here in the midnight silence clutching the Holy Grail of a cup of warm milk.

Scientists have discovered that Mom may have been right after all. Milk contains L-tryptophan, a naturally occurring amino acid that has a tranquilizing effect. Warming it was just Mom's way of making you feel cared for. The natural sleep inducer works just as well cold, or so they say. For me, that bland, childhood warmth is just the ticket. A bit of silence to unwind in; a good book, as soothing as a gentle caress; and a heavy, white mug of warm milk—already I feel sleep rising in my toes, relaxing my feet and ankles and knees. My eyelids are heavy, and the concerns of the day seem too heavy to drag any farther.

I step out to say goodnight to the world at large. A chilly cricket is making himself known by the porch; a heavy, slow transport plane cranks away overhead; and a Hunter's Moon, one slice past full, hangs slightly lopsided in the transparent sky, adding to my wakefulness. It is a tug of war between milk and moon, but it appears milk may carry the contest.

It is true that it is harder to sleep when the moon is full—a throwback to a genetic memory of ourselves as prey and vulnerable, perhaps, but bed sounds good to me now.

SEPTEMBER 9 • *Night*

A compost heap is a busy place at midnight, a Grand Central Station of the garden. The night crew has come on duty and is going about the work of breaking my rough leavings down into rich, crumbly soil. Grass clippings, weeds, leaves, kitchen refuse. These raw ingredients are on their way to becoming earth. By the time they sift to the bottom of the pile they will have lost their individuality to become a corporate entity: humus.

My flashlight finds the wet, pink shine of earthworms big enough to choke a paddlefish. They are engaged in digesting the composting material, further breaking it down and enriching it as it passes through the worms' bodies to become nitrogen-rich castings.

The worms are at the top of their form at night. They are capable of learning simple directions at this midnight point in their circadian rhythm. They can be taught to turn right or left, and they "remember." The same worms, when taught the same trick in the daylight hours, cannot seem to get the hang of it; they are nocturnal beasts.

Cockroaches—welcome here if not in our homes—scuttle over the bits of kitchen waste, their rich, brown color handsome in the light. They, too, are breaking down raw materials. I applaud them at the compost heap and squash them in the kitchen.

Slug trails shine like gossamer in my flashlight beam. These, too, eat and digest bits of waste.

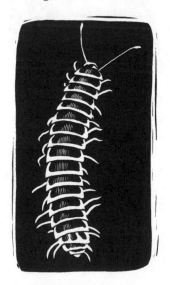

My light catches a quick movement. Lifting a bit of cabbage I find a handsome millipede. He is a herbivore, too, and finds my compost heap a rock-candy mountain of possibilities. This one is orange and dark brownish black. Each of his many segments has a pair of legs. As I turn him over with a stick I find this arthropod looks as if he had a fringe of legs tacked along a center seam. He is a dry-land relative of the lobster, a distant one, surely. The iodine scent of his defensive yellow fluid is strong on the night air.

On a curl of cantaloupe skin I see a huge, black cricket. He has eaten well, apparently. His exoskeleton is as glossy as polished obsidian, and he is the biggest cricket I have seen, with a body fully an inch and a quarter long.

All over the pile, busy as migrant workers at the harvest, are hundreds of pill bugs or wood lice, in all sizes. Some so tiny I can scarcely see them, others to half an inch and then some. Some of these last look odd in my light; they are frosted. They have a whitish, powdery bloom of some sort all over their armored backs. Is it a fungus of some kind or a tiny parasite? They look very pale compared to the glossy gray of the normal wood lice.

Later, in full daylight, I check to see what is active: a few pill bugs hiding from the day, a fly, and near the bottom, the cricket hides in a cavern of grass, still foraging, still growing.

SEPTEMBER 10 • *Night*

A fat garden spider rebuilds her web for the night. Today I noticed there was little of the loosely woven orb left. Something large must have blundered through, tearing it loose from its moorings. If this were the East, I would suspect the kind of brown garden spider that eats its web each morning, only to respin it at night for the hunt. The web's architect was fast asleep in a curled leaf at one end of a remaining guy wire. I could not rouse her even when I tickled what was left of the web with a stick or gently compressed the leaf she slept in.

Tonight the big brown spider is hard at it, tacking new support fibers into place and stitching the loose orb onto them with her spinneret. It takes her only an hour to completely rebuild, an almost unbelievable task when you consider the number of separate steps involved. As I watch, she swings across thin air to lay the first of her spokes. When she is finished, there are eighteen in all, counting from the center to the edge—nine bits of silk from the spider's point of view. When she finishes with this superstructure, she begins the web. I counted forty-two revolutions for an amazing total of seven hundred and fifty-six "stitches" to build this single orb web. As she works, she is as oblivious to my presence as she was when she slept in the curled leaf. Only when she is completely done and poised at the ready is she alert, focused intently on possible prey. When my warm breath hits her, she goes wild, springing back and forth on her flexible web so rapidly she swings herself in circles, blurring before my eyes. A startling explosion of activity for a spider that had earlier refused to respond to my overtures at all.

SEPTEMBER 11 • *Night*

An odd butterfly, or moth, forages in my cat's bowl tonight, feeding on bits of meat or looking for salt or moisture. Its wings are pale tan and shaped like graceful and elegant leaves. They are like those of a curve-

toothed geometer moth, but this one holds them upright over its back like a butterfly. It is near midnight. Is this a butterfly disturbed from its sleep or a nocturnal moth doing what comes naturally—except when it comes to wing position? My copy of *Butterflies and Moths of Missouri*, by Richard and Joan Heitzman, shows such a hybrid-looking creature. It is a goatweed butterfly, which feeds, among other things, on animal droppings and—one might suppose—cat food leavings. Sometimes my lack of knowledge makes my mood as black as the night.

SEPTEMBER 12 • *Early*

The tree is fully leafed with sound. It pipes and whistles and *ok-a-leees* in a cheerful dawn cacophony that is music to me. Gregarious red-winged blackbirds have joined with others of their clan to head southward in huge flocks. They move through the air in clouds and, where they land, they are so densely packed as to create a health hazard in some areas.

It seems early for this particular sign of migration. After raising their young in their bustling adjacent territories in the reeds, they disappeared for a while to molt as if shy of being seen without their handsome plumage. A few have returned to the fringe of marsh at Rocky Hollow, but they did not seem ready to migrate just yet. Perhaps this black, singing treeful of birds is from farther north where the mercury has already dropped the hint to travel southward.

I stand under the tree, grinning like a Cheshire; I never feel the seasons change without this auditory *finis* loud in the air overhead.

SEPTEMBER 13 • *Evening*

A praying mantis hides among the wreckage of my garden. Its pious "hands" folded in prayer do not fool me for a minute. It is out for prey.

Large, round compound eyes survey everything, not missing a trick. In the dying light, her eyes deepen in color; it is her particular adaptation to darkness. Pigment migrates outward to aid sight. In strong daylight the rhabdom of an insect's eye is protected by this pigment. As the pigment changes, more light is able to enter the rhabdom, and this nocturnal creature is still able to hunt efficiently.

And so she does. Her unfortunate mate happens by as I watch. He is smaller and seems to be interested in procreation. She is not. So carnivorous is she that she captures him in those strong forelegs and proceeds to devour him like a stalk of celery. I swear I can almost hear the crunch as she bites into his big green head.

Sex among the insects is a dangerous thing, as dangerous as with spiders. The female is as likely to eat her male as to mate with him, though generally, she prudently does these things in proper insect order. Mate first, then dinner.

SEPTEMBER 14 • *Evening*

Nightfall comes earlier each evening. It seems only yesterday I sat on the porch at 10:00 P.M. and watched the last of the light leach from the sky. Tonight it has been full dark for two hours longer.

It may still be summer by the calendar, but the air smells of fall. The cool, fresh nights feel that way, too, and it awakens something anesthetized by heat and humidity. It feels good. I feel alive—no longer drugged by the effort it takes to move my own body from here to there, but lighter, quicker, easier in all my parts.

SEPTEMBER 15 • *Late night noises*

Sometime in the night, something disturbs the daytime crows on the hill. They squawk and rattle and caw frantically in the darkness. I sit bolt upright in bed, startled into full wakefulness by the impossible sound of crows at midnight. And then I realize what is happening. It is the ancient feud between these big black birds and the barred owl that lives on the hill. When the crows find him in the daylight, they mob him relentlessly and hound him from tree to tree, giving him no rest. Now, he is getting back his due. He has found the crow's nocturnal perch, and he has picked one off with an explosion of sound and black feathers.

The summer insects are still loud in the grasses around the abandoned garden where I search for signs of crow. Crickets seem intent on leaving their outdoor habitat and investigating mine. Every day one or two finds a crack I have missed with the caulking gun, pushes brazenly in, and begins his adventure.

In China it is considered the greatest of good fortune to have a cricket in the house. Tiny bamboo cricket cages house their good-luck charm. In earlier times, these cages were fashioned from porcelain, jade, and ivory—a grand castle for a lowly backyard insect. A cricket on the hearth is good luck in many cultures. They are still kept for that purpose in Portugal, Italy, and Spain. It is a symbol of hearth and home in our own early culture as well. I remember a cast-iron, cricket-shaped bootjack from colonial times. It would be a huge cricket indeed that could help you off with your riding boots. The nocturnal Jerusalem cricket is a virtual Arnold Schwarzenegger of crickets; he might just manage it.

In China, crickets were kept for their fighting abilities as well as their songs. They were fed rice and nuts and mosquitoes that were fattened by the blood of the cricket master's arm. Apparently a blood sacrifice was considered worthy of these miniature warriors. Certain perks were afforded the owner of a particularly fierce cricket. A famous insect named Genghis Khan picked up a tidy sum for his owner in a single match.

According to the *Audubon Society Field Guide*, the true house cricket, *Achela domestica*—a smallish brown affair—lives indoors and emerges at night to look for vegetable refuse. The black, shiny bandits that invade my home to sing under my bed are field crickets (*Gryllus pennsylvanicus*) looking for warmth against the coming autumn chill. They are the same ones who vandalize my late tomatoes and investigate the cat's bowl at night. The rascals are still interested in mating, this late in the year. They may think they can overwinter in my house as if they had gone south.

I can stand the raucous mating calls in the next room. I pretend they are just outside the window by my bed. But when they sneak beneath my closed door and serenade us as well as their intended, I begin to go slowly crazy. Their high trilling is near the upper limits of human hearing at 17,000 vibrations a second—and definitely close to the limits of human endurance. The decibel level is amazingly close to a jackhammer, at least in its effect on my sleep. Who would think such noise could be generated by rubbing those stubby forewings together?

My midnight cricket hunt becomes a test of skill, patience, and endurance. I stalk my prey on hands and knees behind the bureau and under the bed. When I get near, he is silent. It almost seems as if he can read my mind and knows where I am going next. He can certainly throw his "voice," an insect ventriloquist of the first order. This cat and mouse game may last fifteen minutes; longer, if I give up and go to bed after an extended period of silence. Just as I begin to drift off he jars me awake to begin the game all over again.

When I catch the intruder, I treat him with the respect due a worthy opponent. I summarily banish him to the cooling night his fellows already face, just beyond my back door.

It has been a long night, active with owls and crows and crickets—hard on a diurnal creature like myself!

SEPTEMBER 16 • *9:30 P.M.*

Red, green, red, green; not a traffic light here at the edge of the woods but the eyes of some small nocturnal hunter reflecting our headlights. As we approach—or as he turns his head—the angle of light to retina changes, causing his tapetum to light up first red, then green, then back again to red.

We obey the red-light directive and stop as close as we can get to the small graceful creature in our headlight beam. It is a least weasel, rare in Missouri, but sometimes—by sheer serendipity—found in these northern counties.

He is on the way to acquiring a coat of winter white. At first we took his silvery, dark-tipped coloring for just another 'possum out for a ramble. But his long, streamlined form, his quickness, his furred tail, and his size give him away as a weasel, this one in fall molt.

He is our smallest carnivore, and a hungry one at that. (Shrews, with their immense appetite for worms and bugs and their larvae, are considered insect eaters rather than flesh eaters; they are not called carnivores, generally.) A least weasel will eat more than half his body weight in a single day. At nine and a half inches from nose to tail tip that amounts to about a mouse and a half a day.

He just came from his burrow in an old mole run. The fierce little interloper probably frightened the tunneler away, or ate it. Not content with the decor, the weasel added a nest of cornsilk and mouse fur. If the former occupant of the den was a field mouse, that creature may have acted as decorator instead.

The weasel has no intention of being our evening's entertainment. After a thorough check of the edge of the woods, he undulates off, stage left, with that peculiarly graceful, snakelike gait and leaves us wanting more.

SEPTEMBER 19 • *6:30 A.M.*

The sky is beginning to lighten at this hour. It fades to a lovely ultramarine, and only Mercury and Jupiter, steadfast planets, are left shining white in the sky to mark the night. Dawn is reluctant to show its face in late September. The seasons are changing visibly, day by day. It is forty degrees, but the predawn stillness is like a magnet.

The moon is just rising, horns up and only a thin paring of light—the last shavings of the old moon. It is like a fine porcelain bowl worn thin by use and time. The rising sun will shoulder the moon through the sky until it disappears in that bold light, too tired to stake its claim on the day as a fuller moon might. We will have to look sharp to see it at all, a wee fingernail scratch in the blue. Three days from now the moon will be new, a wisp of skin forming alongside the dark shadow.

By 7:00 A.M. the sky has lightened again by half to a wash of pale cobalt. A tender mauve encircles the horizon, reaching to meet in the west.

A few birds are stirring, but only greet the day with occasional *cheeps* and *cherks* and no territorial arias at all. These terse hints of song are not enough evidence to tell starling from sparrow, robin from wren.

By 7:30 A.M. the sun paints Siloam Mountain to the west with a buttery light, though I cannot see it yet for the rim of hills on the east. Crows discuss the day like old men talking politics, planning revenge on the owl, and swifts slice the air with Ginsu wings, looking for early morning insects.

EARLY AUTUMN

The Best of Times

THE NIGHT SCENT CHANGES and takes on a wonderful, cool richness, a complex dimensionality, a tang as redolent as a Chinese tea factory. We breathe the welcome coolness deep into our lungs. I feel it blow throughout my body like a fresh breeze, carrying away the last of summer's heat and humidity, winnowing my cells. There is a sense of change, of fulfillment; the time is now. I feel light enough to fly.

The air itself crackles with freshness and excitement. Drying, dying leaves fill the air with their frostbitten messages.

An autumn night is as noisy in its way as a summer one, if not in decibels, then in the complexity of the cryptic whispers I hear if I listen closely enough. There is a Black Forest cake of sound on the air, layered, dense, and almost too sweet. The crackle of drying leaves underfoot allows no secrets; nothing can walk silently now. Coyotes, foxes, opossums, and raccoons rattle through the brush; mice and voles mark their smaller auditory maps with territorial boundaries. Even woolly bear caterpillars and wood lice cannot go silently in this noisy darkness. I hear their migrations as they shoulder aside the papery leaves, looking for a place to hole up.

Watch the face of the full moon. There are ribbons of Canada geese and the first of the snow geese on their long journeys southward. We listen to their wild gabbling in the night with a chill; of pleasure or of pain, we are never quite sure which.

Other small migrants fill the air with sound; passerines arrow toward wintering grounds in the south throughout the dark hours as well as in full daylight; seed eaters feast at dusk and dawn. Flycatchers and warblers are fly-by-nights; they must hunt in the daylight hours. Swifts and swallows eat on the wing. Insect eaters adapt in many ways to the hardships of travel.

After first frost, Indian summer weather brings warmer nights as well as days that feel more like July than September or October and, with these warm fronts, come changeable weather. There are threats of tornados—a reprise of spring—and a sense of edgy anxiety to spice the mellow days and nights of autumn. There is a price to pay for change.

Wood smoke is like wine on the air—campfires, the first home fires in wood stoves and fireplaces, the backcountry scent of burning brush and leaves—is a good scent. We are aware of the growing problem of air pollution. We buy our wood stoves with an eye to reduced emissions. But still, wood smoke is the smell of home.

Dusk comes earlier, dawn later. The night offers more of itself for us to experience with all our senses. It is a feast of scents and sounds and sights and feelings. Memories seem no more than skin deep in fall; they catch us up suddenly, unaware. Our thoughts hurry to keep pace with the changes. The night is more available, more evocative.

I wrap myself in a favorite jacket and stand dreaming in the crisp night air; I am content, and I know it.

SEPTEMBER 21 • *Dawn*

The growing light shows a sight more familiar in January than the last days of summer: a starling perches on my neighbor's chimney to catch the rising warmth. He is fluffed to almost twice his size to make his own portable insulation. His feathers fill with the warm air of an early furnace, and he is warmer still. The air he captures in those extended breast feathers is nature's own down jacket in action.

SEPTEMBER 22 • *Night*

We visit a strange and familiar country when we walk the park road in the dark of the moon. By day this same stretch is as comfortable to me as my own face in the mirror. At night it is as if I am dreaming of a place I know, but something is not quite right. It seems foreign, exotic, eerie, and just a bit frightening. Exhilaratingly so.

We stand and look over the bridge. We strain our eyes to see what makes the silver streaks in the dark water. The streetlight up the hill just catches the edge of a ripple. There is a lot of action down there. Fish feeding? Insects? Waterstriders? We do not have a flashlight; it remains mystery. A loud splash just upstream startles us—the muskrat, perhaps, or the deer I see near the river.

Harris disappears into the daunting blackness of the park road. There are no streetlights here, only the intermittent shafts of light from homes across the river and the faint stain of light from the moonless sky. It is darkest here where the trees meet overhead—a cave of night. I hurry to catch up.

We put on our night legs, an odd way of walking to absorb unseen obstacles—knees slightly bent, toes up. And it works. In this darkest mile I feel the jarring *whump* of only one pothole, though later our headlights reveal hundreds of holes and hummocks.

We can see only the pale blur of the road and the bottomless sky overhead. Everything else is charcoal and black and indigo, amorphous shapes in the night defined by that starlit sky.

It is beautiful and exotic, but oddly welcoming here. The only thing I fear is the evidences of civilization. We walk an unlit, winding road. If a car comes barreling around a curve, will the driver see us? Can we dodge quickly enough? A pickup truck pulls into a shelterhouse and sits there, lights on, engine running. The door opens and a huge Doberman leaps out, sniffing the ground, anxious for action. Heart in throat, I hope his action is not us; I know he must hear our steps here in the loose gravel. I can hear him snuffling and snorting, pacing avidly.

It is a different country in the night, but I know it well. The soles of my feet tell me where I am. The gravel at the edge of the road keeps me from losing my way in the blind caves under the trees.

My other senses are willing volunteers to map the night. Here is the cold spot on the road where an underground spring mitigates summer's heat and intensifies winter cold. My skin is a giant sensor, telling me where I am, how far I have gone.

I hear the first small riffle in the creek that runs beside the park road. It is muffled by water willows. The second chuckles over exposed rocks in a sharper descant. The third hurries past a small island in midstream with a quick, soft rustle.

An acorn falls from far up in the layers of leaves, banging and *shuushing* through limbs and foliage to *thwack* sharply on the ground where it rolls. I can plot the angle of the hill to the south by the sound and speed of its rolling.

The corduroy rustle of water-loving sycamores to my right would tell me the location of the stream if I were plunked down and spun until I lost all sense of direction. The oaks and hickories of the old-growth forest whisper a different story.

Scents, accentuated by night, act as guides as well. I can smell the rich, wood scent of the big clump of white oaks near the old bench. The creek itself is unmistakable. Its odor crinkles my nostrils pleasurably, and I raise my head to sniff the air like an animal. In the open area tucked back into the forest on the hill, the park's caretakers have been busy. I smell the rich, evocative scent of freshly cut grass and gauge by its faint odor of drying that it was mowed early in the day.

My senses are sad things compared to those of the nocturnal creatures of the forest and river, but how much sharper they are in the dark when I pay attention and respect them. This strange country of night feels like home by the time we see the dim shape of our car in the distance.

SEPTEMBER 23 • *Night*

There is movement in the headlight beams of the car ahead of us. It takes only a moment to decipher the dashes and quick brown dots beside the quiet country road—a mother raccoon leading her babies out for a practice run. I sit up straight in the passenger's seat, alert as a 'coon dog, delighted with the simple chance to hunt with my eyes alone..

Raccoons give parental care for a long time. This one has had the normal early litter of five babies, and they are large enough now to toddle after her on their own, no longer toted by the nape of the neck like kittens, no longer chased up a tree when danger threatens. May born, they are ready for adventure and practice at being out on their own. I detect a swagger.

They stayed close to the den for two months or more, venturing at first only to peer from the hollow in the old snag with alert, shiny eyes. The mother, fully thirty-five pounds but looking thin after nursing this boisterous bunch, has led them out to explore her home territory. I can't wait to get closer. They have that same kind of childish excitement about them as kindergartners on their first field trip.

It will be their last. The car ahead of us is filled with young men with perhaps a bit too much liquid courage in their bellies. We watch them with growing alarm as they weave back and forth across the center line and toss beer cans. Now the car swerves, deliberately aiming for the raccoon family. I am suspended in nightmarish slow-motion; I hear nothing but the revving engine and the repeated thumps as the mother raccoon and her babies are hit.

My rage is incandescent, incoherent. My cherished notion of myself as a pacifist receives another mortal blow. I would kill, myself, now, if I had the chance. The senseless, brutal deaths are anathema; like mayhem visited on the perpetrators would seem just.

I am trembling with fury and frustration; I can feel the bile in my throat, and there is no explanation that will make it subside. Why is it that when some of our kind get behind the wheel of a car, every small thing that moves becomes target—raccoons, house cats, starlings, opposums, turtles. It matters little to the one who feels the power and uses it to deal death. Is life really so cheap?

SEPTEMBER 24 • *Early morning*

A huge black and yellow *Argiope* spider has chosen an inauspicious place for her web; she has sewn the back door to the woodbox. She was not there last night when I fed the cats, and her web is very impressive indeed this morning. She must have worked hard to construct it.

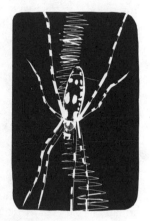

It is an orb web, but with this spider's characteristic heavy white webbing in the center. The male makes the zigzag ladder across the orb; I do not see him. I did not see her until I had opened the door and stretched the flexible web almost to breaking. It must have an amazing amount of tensile strength to stretch so far. And so it does. I have read that for its size, spider silk is stronger than steel. The spider clambered away in a panic, long legs moving almost in a blur. She will look for a better place before stringing her net here again.

I normally see these spiders in the garden. They seem to prefer the tomato plants as supports for their silken ladders, a better choice by far than my active back door.

SEPTEMBER 26 • *Early*

A storm blew up in the wake of last night's warmth and clouds. After sunset the sky muttered with thunder, and in the night it burst on us like a summer storm, like a balloon just too full of water to bear. Heavy rains caused flash flood warnings all over the Midwest. When we got up to survey the damage the street was like a small river, full from curb to curb.

This odd warmth brought fall-fruiting mushrooms of all sorts to the yard and to the woods. Season, rain, and temperature seem to play a part in just what appears, that and the capricious nature of mushrooms in general. The first year we moved to town, a giant stinkhorn appeared by the front walk, erect and obscene and green with slime. It had attract-ed a cloud of insects as if it were rotting meat—just what that "stink" is meant to do. The fetid smell attracts flies to this green jellylike substance, where the spores are borne. The flies carry them away to be dispersed in their droppings.

Other times, deadmen's fingers have pushed up through the dry, parched earth like living stones. We have had a procession of shaggy manes of various types through the years and a sprinkling of big, white field mushrooms—a ubiquitous *Lepiota*.

Now I am waiting to see just what the small hillocks with the emerg-ing russet domes have to offer. You cannot tell the mushrooms from the earthworm castings without getting down on hands and knees in the wet grass for a closer look. Is there a toast-colored cap under that miniature mound or a tunnel?

SEPTEMBER 27 • *Night*

We finally cut down the volunteer Norway-maple sprout in the yard. It was resting heavily on the high-voltage wires from the street to the house, and common sense prevailed against my protests.

Tonight I went out to say goodbye—and to tender a final apology to the truncated stumps that remain—and saw that they glistened and moved in the dark. The stumps looked like a beaded dress worn by a 1920s flapper.

I got my flashlight to closer inspect the moving river of ants produc-ing the odd phenomenon. They were tiny lined acrobatic ants, each no more than a sixteenth of an inch long; there must have been millions. The tree had had several trunks, and each had its stream of shiny brown beads traveling up and down incessantly.

Ants communicate by smell. I wonder if one lone ant discovered the thin, sweet sap and went back to the nest with the information. Then another ant agreed to check it out, then another, and another until the whole tree was covered with ants, each passing information on to the next like particularly juicy gossip.

I zeroed in on a single ant and watched him from the bottom to the top and back. Each time he passed an ant on its way back down, they paused, waved antennae briefly, then resumed their journey. He must have held fifty of these quick confabs on the way up.

When he got there he did as all the others had before him: wander briefly along the edge where the sweet, sap-filled cambium layer is, then work his way back down the trunk, pausing to pass on his own impressions to the ants just making the ascent, antennae moving madly. Are they collecting miniscule amounts of sap or simply surveying the damage?

The cut ends of the downed limbs have only a few ants each. I wonder if there was an aphid farm high up in my maple, and these are the cutoff caretakers? Can the river of ants be surveying the wreckage of the highway that led to their ranch? I look closely at the leaves and find no undue concentration of aphids, only a few here and there, no more. What can the answer be?

SEPTEMBER 29 • *Early*

Something happened while I slept last night. The rumors of fall spread by the early turning poison ivy and sumac—just hints and whispers, really—are suddenly spread like a prairie fire. Up on the hill I can see reds and oranges and yellows in the early morning light, where yesterday there were only subtle variations in summer's uniform green, variations that tell us that *something* is about to happen.

And it did. Sunny days, cool nights; the signal has been given, and the change has begun. The trees have formed hard abscission layers where leaf stems meet twigs. No more nutrients or moisture can pass from tree to leaf. Photosynthesis is a thing of the past in a single night—at least for these first anxious changelings.

The green, so ever-present spring and summer, has disappeared in spots that spread like a stain on a linen cloth all over the north face of Siloam Mountain. The crayonbox colors it hid are bold as a child's drawing.

SEPTEMBER 30 • *Sundown*

Last night at this time it was night only under the trees; the sun still lit their crowns with gold and painted the long east hill beside Fishing River with color. Tonight—and each night—the sun slips into the pocket of night a bit earlier.

I have taken a long walk at sundown for the last two nights—to save my sanity as much as anything. Too many deadlines, too much responsibility, too many opposing pulls on my time and attention, just now, for peace of mind. At least that was the case *before* I gave myself permission for these solo walks. Already, endorphins popping, I feel more myself—calmer, stronger. I like the feel of long muscles working, of walking through puddles of night in this dusky light.

The sky, at least, is still day. Mare's tails of altocumulus clouds sweep the sky, painted pink by the invisible sun. The earth has sunk into its own deepening shadow.

I stand at the old half-moon bridge and look into the still pool below. The bright sky is reflected there like a jewel among the subdued earth tones—lapis and turquoise and coral pink. A small water snake makes his erratic way toward the big fallen tree just below the bridge. His normally sinuous wake seems interrupted by indecision—he goes this way, then that. At last he comes to rest on a submerged limb, and I can see only his tiny head above the water, a dark spot in the glowing sky water.

The pool appears still and glassy, though I know the river's current runs silently beneath the unruffled surface. I stand on the upstream abutment looking down into stillness. There are clouds suspended in that mirror of water that I cannot see when I look at the sky; light is polarized, often, in the northern and southern hemispheres at sunrise and sunset. If I wore polarized sunglasses the clouds would appear by magic.

A muskrat appears in the cloud-filled mirror. He is swimming toward his den under the fallen tree. He cuts through the water gracefully, gracefully for a swimming meat-loaf shape, in any case. His flattened tail rudders behind him, as sinuous as the snake. It is an odd apparition swimming in the sky beneath my feet, and I am dizzy on the old bridge. The strangeness of it—and the angle—upsets my equilibrium, and I nearly tumble into the creek.

OCTOBER 1 · *Day into night*

I spent a long day helping a friend cut cane. It is wonderful weather for the work. This morning, when we began, frost was still on the sorghum, and my hands were stiff at their unaccustomed task. A cane knife is long and sharp like a machete. The cutter wields it as if hacking through the jungle. Whack! Whack! Two strokes—more if you are amateur—to cut away the side leaves, and one more to cut the tall plant just above the ground.

Bend and straighten, bend and straighten down the long rows with their russet seed heads. Later, these seed heads are guillotined off with a machine that looks amazingly like my studio paper cutter. Off with their heads; a huge bundle of stalks at a time lose theirs in a bushel basket. They are fine feed for hogs or chickens or backyard feeder birds; nothing goes to waste.

The stalks are put through the press, and the gears are adjusted to ever closer tolerances as the fresh, green juice is squeezed from the sorghum—the equivalent of maple sap for a Down Easter. And from here the process is the same. A great flat pan of liquid boils down over a hardwood fire. We sit watching into the evening and night, swapping stories, joking, teasing, nursing blisters on hands more accustomed to typewriter keys than cane knives.

Making maple syrup is hard work in the worst of weather. Hands freeze and boots slip in the melting snow, dumping hard-earned buckets of sap at your feet. Sorghum suits my taste in any number of ways. It is a less refined, more ribald product—thick and unsubtle—but oh, the perfect sorghum-cutting days, the perfect sap-boiling nights.

OCTOBER 2 • *Night*

Deep in the night the temperature tailspins to freezing and below as an Alberta clipper sails through from points north. It is an unusual temperature drop from such a pleasant, warm day: no rain, no clouds, just this thin, cold high.

I am awakened by the house exploding around me, a sound I expect in the deep cold of January after the winter solstice brings weather extremes but hardly in early October. Loud cracks and bangs sound like the sap freezing in winter trees, but it is my bedroom walls and ceiling instead. The wood shrinks suddenly and pulls against nails with a sound very nearly as loud as the ones made when the nails were driven in nearly a century ago. At 2:00 A.M., with no competition, it sounds louder still.

As always, I inspect for damage and find none. I expect to see cracks where the bedroom has separated from the rest of the house, fallen away and tumbled into the yard, dumping us summarily from our bed onto the frosty earth. We keep it cooler for good sleeping; as yet we have a window opened a crack. Perhaps the difference in temperatures is what seems to localize these small-hour explosions on cold nights.

After five or six such rifle-shot reports, I am awake and wander outdoors to inspect the glittering cold. The stars look as icy as January in the black sky. There is a fine frost over everything. My bare feet feel burned by its cold.

The smell of smoke from my own fire on the permeating chill is comforting as bed covers. The rich, winey aroma is home. It smells like bourbon-scented pipe tobacco and not like oak and hickory at all.

OCTOBER 3 · *Night*

At 2:30 A.M. the world is nearly silent under the watching stars. No katydids, no snowy tree crickets, no nightjars. Only one lone field cricket braves the chill, and he sounds as if he can barely work up a song, as if he has no hope of an answer. It is a melancholy sound after summer's lovely cacophony. There *is* no silence in summer; school is out and so is every chirping, clicking, singing, stridulating creature that walks, crawls, or flies. But after our record-breaking cold the last two days, the symphony is reduced to a solo.

Only two days ago I saw a snowy tree cricket jitterbugging down one of the long boards in a park picnic table. In a Disney nature film his progress would be accompanied by a comical percussion. He was active

enough in late afternoon. If the nights warm up we will hear that high, clear note in the trees again. And if we do, this lovely, transparent-winged male may just attract a female this late in the game. And if he does, by that continuous high trilling, the female will nudge him until he shuts up, then mate with him. It is not too late. Eggs overwinter, in any case. The female excavates a series of tiny holes and dabs each with excrement. Then she secures the eggs inside and seals them away from the winter cold. Next spring I may see the nearly white nymphs in the trees where they spent the winter.

OCTOBER 5 • *3:00 A.M.*

Fifteen degrees warmer brings a reprise of summer's night music—not as exuberant a cantata, perhaps, but no longer still as death either. The tree crickets have returned as well as a few scratchy field crickets. Even a katydid down the street looks for a last-minute mate.

It is the Leaf-falling Moon, according to an old book of nature lore, and almost full. The sky is as milky as the cup of warm liquid I use as a hedge against insomnia. Far off in the darkness I hear a welcome sound: the high quaver of a screech owl in the woods. The cry of the little seven- to ten-inch owl is suitably eerie.

I cannot imagine why they call it a *screech*. It is more of a sweet, descending whistle with a low trill tacked on the end. If we heard it in the light of day we would call it musical. Because it is of the night—and we are not—it is an "eerie screech."

This one must be taking advantage of the moonlight. Does it really make hunting easier, as it would seem, or is prey more cautious in the Judas light? The owl's huge eyes in that proportionately small face must be able to pick out the least movement as if it were full day. I will not be able to discern his color if he does. My color-sensing abilities faded with the day. His coloring is dependent on locale rather than age or sex or season. Unlike some other birds, he does not go in for that particular quick-change act. This one may be reddish (or rufous); he may be gray brown. You could not prove it by me in the dark. In Missouri we have both, but most likely he is a soft gray like the young owl we cared for in May.

OCTOBER 6 • *Night*

A penumbral eclipse of the moon. Watching it, I feel as if I am underwater, staring up at the moving surface—the underside of the sky. Schools of mackerel clouds slide by overhead, alternately shrouding and exposing the moon. I have come out to watch. This will be a partial eclipse, one that dims the relentless, cold glare of this Hunter's Moon. The clouds are thin and broken, but still hide the moon from view and are stained by its light. They glow like low-

watt bulbs. As the moon's flat disc slices through them, nearing the edge of the cloud bank, they glow brownish, then copper, tinted bloody.

When at last the moon breaks free it is at first startlingly bright. I feel it strike my face like a slap. But as I look I can see that something is not right, not "normal." The lower third is dark, smudged. The light it throws is dirty, stained with the shadow of the eclipse.

And now, at the zenith of darkening, the moon is rusty; the blood-stain will not quite wash out. The dogs have gone mad in the strange bright but sullied light. All over town I hear them baying, crying, howling. The moon has entered the edge of the earth's shadow cone; the darkness thrown on its fullness is incomplete. If it were a total eclipse, the whole of the earth's shadow would block it, eradicate it, wipe it from the cold sky.

TRUE AUTUMN

The Sugar Factory Closes Down

THE NIGHTS EXPAND AGAINST THEIR BOUNDARIES, pushing back abandoned lines of defense. The daylight hours give ground daily, without a fight. The planet tilts to the north, toward the seasonal darkness, and the more intimate dark of night responds, minute by minute. Sunset is suddenly just after 5:00 P.M., then 4:45, and then 4:30 seems barely able to hold onto its faded tatters of light. Dawn comes later by the day.

With the growing dark and cooler weather the last of the leaves turn to scarlet and orange and gold. Their brilliant colors push back the night; the trees look lit from within. But as the last green tree blazes, the first leaves to turn—those impatient adolescents of September—are already dying and losing their hold. They fall to earth to form bright pools like grains of moving sand in an hourglass of seasonal change. In each small green leaf, sugar factories that worked double shifts all spring and summer shut down, turn off the lights, and call it quits for the year. They will retool in the spring. Bare limbs are suddenly stark against the sunset. They are dark-etched harbingers of a season more harsh, more elemental. The night is scented with fallen leaves and with the almost nightly frosts. There is a sense of expectation in the air.

Avian migrants are suddenly urgent. Their voices fill the darkness with a kind of nervous keening. Night after night the face of the full moon is limned with the passage of immense flocks of Canada geese and with the first of the snow geese. If the weather turns Spartan early up north, there may be thousands of these last. But more than likely, in mid to late October the snow geese will simply make a rest stop here in the Midwest and wait for the leading edge of the isotherm of winter to drive them farther south. We may hear their rackety calls for two months yet if fall and early winter are moderate. At dusk and dawn they glean the last of the corn from fields that border on marshlands and ponds or fly for miles to find this yearly bonanza. They return at night to their chosen stopover. Where water stays warmer, near electric or water-treatment plants, thousands of snow geese may take up long-term residence. Near Kansas City these big birds found a home at an ancient water-treatment facility and put on a daily show for local birders.

Retreating armies of small, migrating birds pour across the Midwest. They have passed through for weeks, their small wings stirring invisible currents in the air. We hear their voices against the moon. They bivouac in our trees at dawn.

Crickets invade the house, looking to escape the cold. Those still singing in the grass scratch out a cold song, lower and slower than summer's high stridulations. The silence grows like the thin skin of ice at the edge of a pond. The moon is as cold as the newly frozen earth.

It is a good time for travel, for an escape from the melancholy that seems to pervade like an ink stain. A trip to the desert Southwest, deadly in midsummer, is a delight in October—like turning back the pages of the calendar to taste the sweetness of early autumn all over again. It is a shock to come home to find the frozen pumpkins of Halloween.

There comes a night when we do not see the big groundhog again; he has gone to earth to hibernate until spring. The bats have vacated the airways. They sleep in ancestral limestone caves near the river, caves that bats may have returned to each fall for millennia. Now, humans encroach on these caves and upset the hibernating mammals' cycle. Many are dying, and the bat caves that once held millions may only see a few hundred return.

The bats' prey has disappeared as well—at least seasonally—and the sky seems deserted. The silence grows, its hold on the earth more powerful with each passing night. The chill has taken the night air by the throat and will not let go. It is true autumn. Winter is not far behind. I can smell it on the midnight air.

OCTOBER 10 • *Predawn*

As the light dawns, I admire the morning frost on the pastel earth. Each fallen leaf and blade of grass is embellished with crystals so small, so delicate that if I bend to see them more closely, my warm breath obliterates them instantly. I hold my breath to see these fragile, ephemeral treasures so soon to disappear in the warmth of rising sun. What profligate, transient beauty.

If I were to paint such a magical, miniscule vista, I would be tempted to decorate my work with white pigment—but it would be a mistake. White paint is opaque and heavy. These treasures have been painted with pure light and hung with crystal prisms so small my smallest brush

could not begin to delineate them.
These were done by an artist far
more precise than I will ever
be—and more patient as well.

But no, it is not patience. In a
single night these frost-crystal land-
scapes were painted in broad
strokes, each glittering swath con-
taining billions of exquisite, tiny
jewels. It is not patience—it is
magic. It is the action of water
molecules joined, one by one, with
the fine glue of cold.

OCTOBER 11 · *Night*

The second day of a three-day teaching workshop and I have had little
time to think of anything but tone and value, pigments and watercolor
washes and the balancing of personalities. I am tired and overstimulated
at the same time, and I go into night for a bit of air and silence.

But it is hardly silent. Instead, there is the noise of a thousand creep-
ing, crawling, burrowing creatures moving through the still-crisp fallen
leaves. I thought at first it was raining and stuck out my hand, palm up,
to catch a drop. But as my senses calmed, I could tell the sound was
more constant, moving, changing—a little traveling music.

Woolly bears and crickets, earthworms
and spiders—it is a night migration on an
earth-bound scale. These creatures migrate
downward into the earth.

OCTOBER 12 · *Evening*

The lake at Watkins Mill is a dark, moving reflection of the pewter sky, burnished to a dull
sheen. The clouds scud by overhead, thick and
lumpy as a peat bog.

The dead snag in the middle of the lake
sports a living extension, impossible at first to
identify. The binoculars make sudden sense of

this black, snakelike form. It is the cormorant. He stands at the very end of the snag, facing us. He is alone this late in the year with no mate or companions to keep him company. He looks aloof, haughty with that prehistoric snake neck. What does he care that he is the only cormorant at the lake? His time here is nearly over. He is on his way to the Gulf states and good fishing.

OCTOBER 14 • *Night*

Time after time, nightmare images dangle and dance before my eyes, projected on my retinas by an overactive brain. They fade only when chased by full consciousness, summoned desperately for the task. A green, gourd-shaped object, shiny with fresh blood, hangs suspended in midair; a black noose, attached to nothing, threatens beside my bed. A spider descends his glistening web and stops inches from my face, his huge and menacing abdomen slowly bobbing. It disappears as I stare hard into the darkness.

I am not asleep. These images linger for seconds without end after I have opened my eyes to dispel them. My tired brain has conjured them to get my attention. Slow down. You are operating in nanoseconds, spinning out of control. It is true. I cannot make sense of my life at this speed. Fickle as a summer storm, I bop from project to project, trying to focus on each one as I pass it by, trying to concentrate, trying to convince myself I care.

Snap your fingers. In that brief sound are contained 500 million nanoseconds—the speed computers operate in without effort, the speed we are increasingly caught up in as everything from supermarket check-outs to typewriters to video games are computer run.

Before the thirteenth century, there were no hours—at least in the sense we know them today—nor the power they have over us. In their holy desire to use time to best advantage and to the glory of God, Benedictine monks divided the day into pieces, marked them off, named them, and assigned them duties. Minutes and seconds were afterthoughts that snuck into our reluctant consciousness only recently. I feel them behind me, pushing. I feel their pressure like a tangible force against my back.

But nanoseconds are different. I do not feel them at my back, making me hurry to catch up. They spin before my eyes like subliminal images too fast to assimilate, too fast to make sense of. They invade my brain, racing along neural pathways, shorting out synapses, shooting sparks. My nightmare images are nanoseconds, plucked at random from the melee and projected outward.

I cannot operate at this speed; none of us can. I need to get back to real time, the time contained in the slow, sure growth of an acorn and in its falling—at the perfect and proper time—to earth. Put on the brakes. Shut off the power. Leave the nanoseconds to the microchips. They were built to handle them.

OCTOBER 15 • *Night*

The sweet, rich scent of longed-for rain fills my nostrils like the memory of peace. I feel it gratefully, like the thirsty earth too long without rain.

In the dark I hear the patter and splatter and plop all around me, an orchestra of natural instruments. Rain on leaves makes a soft and muffled percussion. Drops against the lid of the ash can are sharp, staccato. In the drying leaves overhead, the sound whispers. It is a syncopated rhythm that produces a quiet that is almost tangible, a peace I wrap around myself like a blanket.

I love the smell of autumn rain. This one, coming after such a long dryness, is especially sweet and carries in itself the dust of summer, the crispness of leaves, the tang of wet wood.

I hold my hands out to catch the rain; they are pale shapes flattened and featureless in the dim blue light, swimming like blind cave fish. I can feel the drops like kisses, like benediction against my palms, a gift of great price.

On the farm, when these drought-ending rains meant the end of sour, niggling bits of water from our inadequate well, the end of lugging heavy jugs of water from town, the end of washing my hair in the church basement and letting my long braids dry like clammy hawsers against my neck, the rain was welcome as life. The garden welcomed it. Limp leaves that had shrunken in on themselves unfurled, stretched, and plumped before my eyes. The pasture greened again overnight.

When the well meant life to our small herd of goats, our chickens, the two irascible geese, and our contingent of farm cats, nothing was sweeter than the sound of night rain against the dried earth—individual drops slapping hard, singly and audibly. Each was beautiful to me, and precious. I added my own grateful tears.

OCTOBER 16 • *Early evening*

I walk in silence down the long, golden tunnel into evening. The light is failing, and the golden day is chilling down into night, but the walk is therapeutic, calming. The silence is as satisfying as bread. If I walk without a sound into the growing night I will disappear into it without a trace, one with the redolent darkness.

The air is as sweet as a grandfather's pipe, with that same rich, sad scent of leaves and maple and autumn. The drying, aromatic dregs of summer lie on the cooling earth and send their scent up like memories. They recall a friend's story of tea grown in a remote province of China, where it is picked, leaf by leaf, by young virgins; rolled, each leaf singly; and set to dry on silk. Such tea would smell like this perfect evening and taste, perhaps, like satisfaction.

OCTOBER 18 • *Night*

Cooler air is beginning to make more permanent inroads into the Midwest. It is moving in like an invading army and planning, apparently, to bivouac. Yesterday morning and again last night, snowflakes formed in the upper atmosphere where it was colder still and dropped in for a short stay. They hit my windshield wrapped in rain; the splatters they made were coarse, gravelly.

We could not wait to get a fire started. What is left of the woodpile has stayed relatively dry through the fall, but it is going fast. We are down to the last layer, damp with fallen bark and sawdust and beginning to compost.

I am reluctant to use this last bit. On turning over a log I found it encrusted with small, moving, gray scales. Wood lice have found a home here, attracted, one by one, to the dark, to the precious moisture and the promise of food. They may look as communal as ants, but they are individual as fingerprints, drawn to the same perfect habitat.

At least it was perfect until the weather turned cool. The wood sat undisturbed all summer, catching a bit of rainwater from time to time. A falling leaf would sift down between the logs and begin the long, invisible combustion of decay, providing both food and moisture to these small landlocked crustaceans. An occasional dead bug provided protein in the form of small carrion. The cover of the wood was nearby to protect these armadillolike creatures from predators like the ants and millipedes that also make the back porch their territory.

I have read that female wood lice have a pouch much like opossums and other marsupials in which they carry their eggs and newly hatched young. I wonder how many wood lice I have to ambush to see it? I will have to move fast. They roll up instantly when disturbed.

OCTOBER 19 • *Early morning*

When the sun comes peering sleepily over the eastern hill, I wonder if it is still as surprised as I am by the sight that greets it? To the west, Siloam Mountain, that long glacial mound that assumes a big name with a hilly swagger, is as crimson and russet and orange red as a crate of Washington apples. All spring and summer the hill has been green—that tentative green of spring, tender and varied. Then the strong analogous hue of June and July, as intense as dye. Then the mitigating gold greens of August and September, hinting at this chimera change to come, but in no way preparing me for its vivid, paint-box colors. It was still and always green.

For two weeks now the change has been more and more noticeable; every night photosynthesis stops in this tree or that, and the green leaches from the leaves. Overnight this tree or that shows its true colors, free of the masking green of summer.

Among the knock-'em-dead colors are other changes, changes less obvious but more telling than this brash display. I see a few more denuded branches reaching through the leaves each morning. Here and there a bare gray tree rises like smoke against the luminous foliage. I can trace the curve of the hill itself through leaves that only a week ago masked all contours but their own. I can see sky through the upper branches. The more subtle changes warn me that the bright surprise is short-lived. Soon all the leaves will fall at the tree's feet. The limbs will be bare, etched against the sky. The morning sun never seems surprised by the hill in winter, and I have time to get used to it.

OCTOBER 21 · *Night*

The meteor shower falls nowhere near as enthusiastically as the mulberry leaves. Tonight's record cold and hard frost have conspired to turn them crisp and loosen their hold on the twigs. The extra weight of the frost is the last in a long parade of seasonal straws. They rain from the tree with a constant bang and whisper, snatching my attention from Orion in the east.

At only twenty-five meteors an hour, the Orionids are hardly the most active meteor shower in the world; no hurried, harried type-A displays for these laid-back ice balls. The Perseids of August best them by a wide margin. The twenty-degree cold reaches down the neck of my quilted jacket. I will satisfy myself with a few bright 3:00 A.M. flashes and retire to the warmth of the wood stove.

Still, the clatter of falling leaves promises a changed day. By noon the leaves will abandon the trees and leave the branches shivering as I am in the cold air.

OCTOBER 26 · *Desert night*

The desert night is full of stars—so bright, so sharp, so close I could reap a handful from the sky if I swept an arm overhead. My sister and I walk out into the desert for a moment.

Black-tailed jackrabbits fresh from the desert leap and bound like long-legged basketball players in the fine mist of the lawn sprinklers. Members of the hare family, jackrabbits can leap five to ten feet at a shot—twenty, if they are alarmed. They must have tired of their rubbly scrapes among the prickly pear and rabbitbrush and come to town for a taste of the soft life.

Below the town of Henderson, the lights of Las Vegas sparkle and flash like a man-made Milky Way. We just drove their daylight canyons as if we knew what we were about, as if we piloted a meteor through the darkness.

OCTOBER 27 • *Desert dawn*

A fine, mutable light brings dawn over mountains that by themselves change color, hour by hour, through the day, dressing first in palest blue, then violet, then sepia and melon and midnight. As constant as the earth itself, they play at being fickle. Yesterday's dawn was as blue and misty as an August daybreak in Missouri woods. The mountains to the east were only flat, pale shapes—feet lost in paleness. It was as if an Oriental master had painted them with hand-rubbed ink on a long, rice paper scroll and called it Mountain Dawning.

This morning it is the light itself that changes, dressing the high cirrus clouds in melon, rose, deep violet, and the intense golden glow I see only above the clouds, above the earth itself.

The desert mockingbirds cannot stop talking about the dawn. Now, in late October, a thousand migrating relatives pass through, stop to rest, chatter, and head south. I laugh, and wryly. I cannot help but think of last night's marathon talk. Yvonne and I caught up on three years and a lifetime of news and feelings and comically skewed, octoscope visions of a shared and separate past. We sounded like those mockingbirds.

OCTOBER 29 • *4:30 A.M.*

At this hour the night is as silent as I am. I hear only the crunch of my heels on the mixed rocks and pebbles and the cool mountain wind. It investigates the valley at night as if curious about our lives. Coyotes and jackrabbits pass through like smoke, trailing scents of their own.

I had expected the warm night—much warmer than the crisp late October we left at home—to have the same late-summer noises the temperature would suggest: a rusty creak of a cricket or two, a katydid running late, perhaps the high trill of a desert toad. But instead there is only the crunch of my shoes and the fresh-scented wind bringing rumors of sagebrush and creosote bush from the desert caliche (limestone crust) and a whisper of oleander from someone's manicured backyard.

OCTOBER 30 • *Night*

The Nevada night is beaded with hundreds of black, shiny spiders, them-selves decorated with a red hourglass. Poisonous and shy black widows are as common here as *Argiopes* are at home. They spin their messy webs hard by my sister's walk. We have passed them for days now, unaware.

LATE FALL

Winter's Cold Breath down Our Necks

CHANGE IS NO LONGER A SUGGESTION BUT A STATEMENT. The world spins precipitously toward the chill edge of winter and we fall helplessly into its waiting cold. Indian Summer days are forgotten as if they had never been. There is no looking back. No matter that the calendar says the winter will not begin for weeks. This new chill laughs at our calendars and flaunts its power.

I spend as much time as I can in the night, feeling my way toward winter, watching the change, monitoring the seasonal turning. It is rapid and emphatic. Late fall is blood cousin to winter, though there may be an occasional mildness. One Thanksgiving day we walked the trail at Watkins Mill in shirt-sleeves and talked of pitching our tent and sleeping out—no need for down-filled bags. The night was as mild as May.

During a normal November, when autumn turns suddenly cold, hard freezes blacken the last of the tender vegetation. The night air is noisy with crisp fallen leaves and the migrating wings of hundreds of thousands of snow geese. The stars are cold and distant, no longer intimate and friendly as on a hot summer's night. Frost is a nightly occurrence. The nights are cold and damp and cut through my flesh like a stropped razor.

A fire in the stove feels like homecoming in November, the chore of splitting wood suddenly easier in the chill. The wood's fibers are newly obedient. I watch the billets fall crisply to each side of my axe with a satisfying *chonk* and am warmed by the preparations for the night. I lean on my axe handle and admire the transparent sunset and the pile of split wood I have created—stove length and promising comfort.

Other preparations go on all around me. There are few insects left at the streetlights or navigating with the moon; they have laid their plans for another season, building cocoons, laying eggs, secreting themselves between the shingles on my roof. Opossums find their dens and fill them with the abundant insulation of dry leaves and grasses. Snails are sealed into their shells, hidden in the earth. Ground squirrels sleep beneath our feet; it would take hours to wake them from their torpor. In the trees, their larger cousins line their holes with leaves and pull them in after them, wrapping chilly faces in luxuriant tails for the night. The dawn chorus shrinks to a wintry few—chickadees, titmice, cardinals —singing cold songs. The migrating songbirds have beat it southward.

Owls are grateful for the first snow; prey scurries over that whiteness visible as full day. Their young are hunting on their own now. It is a good time to be an owl.

Sunrise is suddenly witchcraft. It lights a crystal world that lasts only an endless, timeless instant until the thin warmth of the sun melts frost and everything is back to normal. One late evening the snow begins in shy flurries—small, hard-crystalled, tentative, but blowing at the last like January. There is more than a hint of what is to come; it is a clearly written preface.

NOVEMBER 1 • *Evening*

The last of the woodchucks has gone to earth for the winter. I saw them feeding at dusk less and less often as the days cooled. Their feeding periods seemed briefer by the day. Now even the youngest and most active animals have retired to their leaf-lined burrows for an odd half-sleep, half-death. Their breathing has slowed to an almost indiscernible effort; the body temperature hovers between forty-three and fifty-seven degrees. So deep is this torpor that it *is* a small death, a comatose state, as if this groundhog had found Snow White's poisoned apple and now lay waiting for the kiss of spring to rouse it. I imagine it lying on its back, paws folded in a story tale parody. In fact, it is more than likely curled into a tight ball to conserve body heat.

He will be out and feeding again—if the weather cooperates— by mid-February, and he will be ready. The woodchuck loses between one-third to one-half his autumn weight as he sleeps. No wonder he fed so voraciously all the long autumn afternoons, making of these forays his own harvest. I watched him snatch at rough grasses and seed heads with handlike paws and eat with total concentration. Instinctively, he knew what he was about: survival.

NOVEMBER 3 • *Night*

Daylight saving time is over; the night has suddenly grown large, devouring chunks of the day before I am ready. I resent the robbery. I feel cheated, disoriented, strange inside my own skin. I wish we would stop legislating time and leave it to its own devices. Let us allow ourselves the gradual accommodation to the shorter days rather than forcing winter down our own throats. I like daylight saving time no more in summer, when sticky, hot days seem never to come to an end.

Tonight a single cricket sings into the evening—a lonely, wistful sound, an emptiness. The full moon fills the sky overhead, taking up the slack. Jupiter hangs below it like a pendant, like a fragment broken away and dangling. The other stars have disappeared, swallowed by the wide-eyed stare of the Mad Moon.

It is the old designation for November's full moon, gleaned from my nineteenth-century book of natural history. This year's *Old Farmer's Almanac* calls it the Beaver Moon, and these flat-tailed mammals *are* active in their urgent preparations for winter. We often see the results of

a night's industry as we walk around the lake at Watkins Mill—trees and saplings tossed to the ground like a giant's game of pick-up sticks. Each morning there are fresh cuttings.

A single beaver makes short work of twenty years' growth or more when he cuts a tree. A 5-inch-diameter willow is down in three minutes. The timber-cutting creature works with his lower incisors, using his upper teeth for leverage and, like most lumberjacks, he works each tree alone. If felling a big tree, though, he may call in help; several may work together. Beavers usually choose 2- to 8-inch trees for easiest cutting and choice building and dining possibilities, but a record 5-foot, 7-inch-diameter cottonwood was felled in British Columbia. The noise must have been deafening as 110 feet of tree came crashing to earth. Once down, it had to have provided a whole colony of beavers with gainful employment: taking leaves and small twigs on the spot and cutting away branches under five inches in diameter to use in building and repairing dams and lodges. The large trunks themselves are abandoned where they fall.

The beavers are usually quiet in their lodges by the time we happen by. They are primarily nocturnal. But in this busiest season—the season of preparation—I may see them if I am still and patient.

Now, I hear only their soft snuffling under their wattle-and-daub roofs of plaited twigs and dark brown Missouri mud. I stand above the lodge at Watkins Mill and listen. The sounds beneath my feet might as well be the wind.

The beavers' lodge is a marvel of engineering; thick, two-foot walls hold my weight easily, but I avoid the thinner roof. I do not want to drop in unexpectedly. I already crashed an escape tunnel, falling into the muck up to my kneecap. I did not know it was there. There may be a network of these tunnels around a single lodge. They lead to water, to food, to safety. And now this one leads to open air and a big-footed human.

But still, the Mad Moon seems better suited somehow to this glare that blasts through bare branches and invades every square inch with its light, seeing everything, tearing away our tenuous privacy with its bold round eye. It is insistent. I cannot escape it, not even indoors. It throws moving rectangles of light in my windows. They creep across the floor from right to left through the night as if scanning, as if memorizing the minute details of my life. Only the beaver's cavelike home is safe from this prying, demanding moon. The beaver builds no windows.

NOVEMBER 4 • *Night*

The leaves have nearly fallen now, crisp and dry as paper. They harbor no secrets. There is an auditory map of every creature that roams the night. I can hear the raccoon fleeing across the backyard and through the abandoned garden and up into the woods. I hear Cougar, the little homeless cat I see only by night, racing to accept my offering, rattletrapping her way through the deep blanket of leaves. I hear Prince, the big husky on the hill, pace at the end of his chain in an endless loop of sound. I can hear the field mice as they look for safe haven in the foundation stones of my house, the opossum lumbering through the darkness, the very breath of breeze that touches my cheek like a tentative finger; it is audible if not visible. The fallen leaves make the darkness penetrable by imagination and surmise. I could not keep a secret if I wanted to.

NOVEMBER 5 • *Night*

The moon is so full it looks about to pop. It is as bright as a search light. All day I watched the pure colors of my kitchen window prism slide across the floor, melt up the walls, sneak down the hall, its rainbow lights tracking the sun and investigating the corners of the house. Will it cast a nightbow as well?

It will. I take it to the yard where the moonlight casts etched shadows on pale, dry leaves. I find the purest, brightest patch of light to stand in, and there it is. Dancing on the white folds of my nightgown, the dusky nightbow moves with my outstretched hand. The colors are subtle, muted. I see more rusty reds and purples and maroons and siennas than daylight's blues and greens and oranges. But there it is, nonetheless. A nightbow in my lap, a caught prize, magical and moving.

Extended exposure photography has proven that there is no shortage of red light in the moonlight. Photos taken of red flowers by night are as colorful as any full sun shots, if the film is sufficiently exposed. Perhaps these lovely lights from my small prism are proof as well, though more in the nature of a suggestion of red than a bold-faced statement.

NOVEMBER 6 • *Night*

The sky seems too empty now, almost lonely in its wide void—no chimney swifts, no nightjars, no small, flittering bats. These last have left the airways to hibernate in ancestral limestone caves or in man-made mines that worm throughout much of Missouri like holes in Swiss cheese. Largely abandoned, these were the coal and lead mines of the earlier part of the century. Only the bats use them now. They have vacated the smaller nursery colonies in derelict buildings and other more widely spaced nesting cavities—in trees, small-town buildings, our own outbuildings and attics. Most of us who live in urban or suburban areas cannot imagine the numbers of bats we share the night with. They are nearly silent, after all, and much smaller than nightmare paints them.

The bats have summered in their smaller colonies, mating and feeding nightly in territories as intimate as the air space between two houses. Now, in the stony caverns they use as communal winter roosts, they sleep by the millions, like vertical shingles suspended from the roof. Their body temperature is as cold as the rock of the cave walls; their

breathing and heartbeat slow. Like the woodchucks, the bats have entered their long winter's sleep. They will rouse themselves only if a protracted warm spell wakes their insect prey—or if, during the long night of winter, small bladders fill too full to bear. We share that much, at least, with these most feared of nocturnal mammals.

There are seventeen species of bats that populate Missouri nights with leather-winged movement, darting this way and that in pursuit of insect prey. Tonight there is not a one to see. Perversely, I miss the little monkey-faced creatures. They are only too little understood, the victims of unexamined prejudice.

NOVEMBER 7 • *Evening*

The deer—six, no seven of them—stand nearly invisible at the edge of the forest. They have traded their lightweight summer coats of warm tan for insulated gray brown, each hair hollow to hold body heat close in. Not only hollow, these coarse, rough hairs are chambered and water-repellent. It is an efficient adaptation to the coming cold and to the demands of camouflage.

These winter coats are countershaded like summer's lighter pelts—darker hair above and lighter on the belly. Like many mammals, deer benefit by this countershading to become nearly invisible to the careless eye. Darker hairs of the back blend with the cast shadows of trees and branches; the lighter undercoat seems to average out the shadow cast by the deer itself. It works all too well on those days when we only have time to drive through, hurried and distracted. Unless I take the time to look, really look, until I let myself begin to see, the winter woods remain as bare as imagination suggests.

Now the deer are the same color as the late-fall woods, the same dun of fallen leaves and bare twigs—a gray, a tan, a non-color that blends without a shadow. I can see these only when one lifts a head to look at me. The moving spot of moist black catches my eye like an anomaly, a game of nature's own: "What is wrong with this picture?" I count the big mammals in the gathering dusk by counting triangles, those dark arrows of two bottomless black eyes and a velvet nose. Connect the dots; there is deer.

The seventh gives herself away in the jigsaw of ripstop oak leaves and branches by another kind of motion. Her back is to me, her head down, the triangle hidden. But a quick shake of that white-flagged tail gives me bearing on her position in the darkening woods. It shines like a candle.

And at last they will put up with my rude staring no longer. One snorts and bounds away, white flag waving like a banner. The rest follow, showing their colors at last: no surrender, but banners flying nonetheless. I am suitably chastened and stand looking after them like an outcast.

NOVEMBER 9 • *Sunset*

Iridescent turkey wings catch the coral of sunset in their barbs and barbicels. One by one the big brown-black birds cross the road in front of us, catching us by surprise.

Hunters insist the wild birds are ghosts, wood spirits able to appear and disappear at will. I am inclined to go along with them. We had just driven the small loop by the picnic grounds. We saw nothing through the bare woods but more woods—underbrush stripped of leaves, understory buck naked against the trunks of the larger trees, and everything as leafless as fence posts. A lovely and subtle gray-sienna-lavender sets the color scheme for November woods, with a few bright touches of scarlet or yellow where a single stubborn leaf clings to its twig. There is no place for a twenty-pound bird got up in gloss black to hide—except that obviously there was. The three birds, a big tom and his two smaller hens, appeared before our eyes as if by avian magic, and we were as surprised by the last as by the first.

I knew they traveled in small family flocks. I expected more birds to appear after the big male, and when they did, when they materialized out of nothing, I was as startled as if I had not expected their coming.

They disappeared just as completely, just as silently, on the other side of the road. Wings spread (Madame Butterfly's own fantails nearly three feet across) they half-ran, half-flew before us. We watched them as intently as I have watched a cabbage looper on my own arm, and suddenly they were simply not there. Gone without a sound.

NOVEMBER 11 • *Midnight*

A thick frost has formed, crisp as the fallen leaves and blades of dead grass it covers. It is so cold it feels hot to my bare feet, as if I burned myself on coldness. It disappears instantly where I step. My passage is marked in the starlight by dark prints against the pale, frosty ground.

One night a year I like to walk barefoot in the frost. The almost burning cold reminds me how close opposite sensations, conditions, or emotions may be. Fascination is just at the far edge of revulsion. There is sadness in joy. Love and hate look in a mirror to find each other. Life and death are themselves not so far apart; one endlessly becomes the other. "Remember that you are but dust, and to dust you shall return," the priest tells us on Ash Wednesday. Yes, but from that dust a new life may form. My cold, burning feet remind me of that truth.

NOVEMBER 14 • *Night*

I can smell the frost forming. It prickles in my nostrils. Perhaps it is only the cold and a hint of skunk on the air. One has been snuffling around the edges of the garden in search of a handout. I smelled its perfume—too close for comfort—when I opened the basement door.

Mephitis mephitis is the Latin name for the ubiquitous striped skunk; it means "bad odor." And apparently someone felt the need to be emphatic—bad odor, bad odor!

Winter sleep will be intermittent for these handsome mammals; unlike true hibernators, they will not bother to turn down the internal thermostat. When the temperature outdoors rises above fifteen degrees, we may find ourselves face to face with a foraging bundle of *mephitis*. If it gets colder than that the skunk will stay denned up in a sort of stupor.

NOVEMBER 15 • *Sunset*

The western sky caught fire in an instant. The overcast lit up, stained scarlet as the sun finally slipped beneath the day-long gray. A sudden flash of crimson tints everything in its path.

The long drizzle glazes everything with a wet shine. The scarlet runs down into the street and touches the dead leaves and glistening twigs and the sightless windows of our houses with opaque color.

I feel like a child as I walk in the rain in the hot-pink light. I look about me with delight, as if seeing after a long blindness. Late fall sunsets seem more spectacular than those in full summer, if only as an about-face contrast to the gray, wet days. I could not, simply could not send regrets to the invitation of this cellophane-tinted world; it had to be explored. It is too ephemeral, doomed to darkness in minutes. I want to see it *now*.

NOVEMBER 16 • *Night*

I hold continuity in my arms—ancient, angular, bony, purring. My day sleeper staggers to my cozy lap. Her old bones are like a heat-seeking missile this chill night.

Like all cats—wild or domestic—she is nocturnal. Like all cats, she sleeps eighteen to twenty hours out of every twenty-four. But her active hours seem shorter now as she stirs herself after supper to find my warmth. She will stay awhile, purring and kneading like a kitten, imagining me a mother, a great, soft safety. Then she will repair to a chosen nap spot for a few more hours.

Her belly is still on daylight saving time. Her hunger wakes her promptly at 9:00 P.M., exactly the hour I fed her all summer and most of the fall. But now the evening's prime time is still in full swing and not time for news and bed at all.

I fed her and the others and wild Cougar when the late news came on. After the noon news shows and the hour and a half news marathon at 5:00 P.M., I have had quite enough of the world's happenings. So while Harris gets his final fix of the latest for the day, I feed the cats, step outside to see what is what, and ready the coffee for tomorrow. Or I did, until Westport ignored the end of daylight saving time.

She has been with us for almost nineteen years—through the farm years, through small-town adjustments, through the lives and deaths and disappearances of forty cats, more or less. She holds her head cocked at an angle as if she listened for something I cannot hear; she had a stroke years ago. And she loves me with a fierce and stubborn loyalty. Let those who say cats do not love, that they are not faithful like their canine friends, come and meet my Westport.

NOVEMBER 18 • *4:00 A.M.*

I was awakened by a nightmare, shocked to full consciousness at 2:30 A.M. The thin, repeated cry of a dying cat, heard too often this year of feline leukemia, has made its way to my sleeping mind. This time it is only a dream, but a dream disturbing enough to kill all thought of sleep. Warm milk, a good book, and the welcome warmth of the wood stove restore my equilibrium, that and a warm and healthy cat in my lap.

At last the milk does its work, and I begin to think of bed with as much clarity as the emptiness of space. Just to make sure, I step out to find the Leonids, November's meteor shower in the constellation Leo.

The meteor shower peaked last night, hidden modestly behind heavy cloud cover, but there are stragglers until the twentieth of the month. Look quick, there in the east-northeast—a bright needle of light pricks the night sky. At five meteors an hour, the Leonids are too sluggish by far to wait for here in the cold; it catches my breath and reaches chilling fingers down my neck. It is close to freezing, and my body has not adjusted to the seasonal change. The stars hang in glistening, transparent curtains, sharp as pinpricks, but none of them moves. I watch until the cold sucks the last of my nightmare out with my body warmth and return to my bed at last.

NOVEMBER 19 • *Nightfall*

Great flocks of starlings gather in the trees by the river at dusk. In the late fall they abandon their separate holdings to form roosting flocks near the river.

They move against the sky in unison, as if choreographed in their synchronous flight. We watch as they approach the big cottonwoods that fringe the banks of the Missouri River. They fall from the sky like rain, each bird alone and yet all together.

When the flock has landed at last and settled in, noisy and creaking, the trees look fully leafed in black and moving as if stirred by a gentle wind.

NOVEMBER 21 • *Sunset*

A field of dead and weedy goldenrods stands frosty against the dying light of the sun, backlit and glowing. Each one casts a long shadow toward me as though beckoning me forward. Converging shadow lines meet at the sun's transient warmth. They will soon melt indistinguishably into the enveloping earth shadow.

The wind is colder than I thought here by the lake. Knifelike, it cuts through my unlined jacket. It makes my cheeks flame, my nose run, but it clears my head like a stiff, new broom. I had felt as though I were stuffed with cotton, dull as a rag doll left too long on the shelf, dusty and neglected. Out here the tattered stuffing blows away with the remnants of the day, and the blood flows again.

The late fall colors turn rich as if to compensate for the sun's departure, as if to convince the sun to stay. The water's sapphire deepens to lapis. The shadows are deep blue. In the woods on the far bank they are purple, warmed by the brick red and sienna of the oak leaves hanging on as stubbornly as I do. The warm sienna of broom sedge flames in the cellophane light.

The far bank—dull yellow clay—is lit and warmed to luscious butterscotch, and the last green grass makes me think of the green hills of Ireland. The lower the sun sinks, the richer all these colors become, richer, deeper, pulsating as if they would burst before my eyes in the deafening silence. I could never paint it so boldly. Pigments and paper are poor substitutes for a painting done with light and life itself.

NOVEMBER 23 • *Sunrise*

The dawn chorus has shrunk to a few singers, but it seems as loud as ever as the chickadees and starlings and pigeons take up the slack. Starlings do their imitations of hawks and quail and a thousand other creaks and whistles, trying to convince me their name is legion.

And it is. Since they were first released in Central Park in 1890, they have crowded out many of our native bird species. They compete for food and nesting cavities. There may be tens of thousands of birds in a single winter roost; it sounds like that many in my front yard.

NOVEMBER 25 • *Night*

The smell of a cooking fire has made me hungry for one last charcoal-broiled steak. I can taste it already, smoky, succulent, simple.

The briquets burn hot in the growing dark. Tongues of flame lick the last of the burned-on grease from the grill. I scrub the grate with my brush, and a sparkle lights up the night as bits fall into the fire and are instantly consumed like meteorites. The gray and blaze orange of the charcoal fire's surface looks like burning lava.

Far off to the southwest, a tiny shaving of moon seems to point at the place where the sun went down as if to make sure I have noticed. The moon skims low around the horizon now, never rising too far; it will set by the time I go to bed.

This slip of a moon reminds me of something. It is so new, so delicate. A friend cuts her baby's fragile fingernails with small, curved scissors. The fine parings fall to the floor. This small whiteness in the sky is one of those tiny crescents caught up by the wind.

The moon is nearly alone in the sky; only Venus and one or two of the bolder planets are visible now, but it will be a good night for stargazing later. It is as clear as my aunt's wisp-thin crystal goblets.

NOVEMBER 26 • *Dawn*

There was heavy fog last night. The low ceiling has threatened for days, stuffing our wood smoke back down our throats. It finally closed in around our ears after the lovely clear evening. I went out at 3:00 A.M. to check on the world. It was as still and silent and white as if wrapped in cotton wool. The sky's own dampness was on my cheeks like tears. The light from the town tinted the low sky an eerie gray-peach, filling the bowl of night with a strange slurry from horizon to horizon.

And this morning Siloam Mountain wears a white beret; the fog crystallized into sparkling frost just where the vapor hung down over the brow of the hill, becoming solid on the bare limbs. Only the mountaintop is covered with this glittering grayness. It will disappear by 8:00 A.M.

NOVEMBER 27 • *Night*

Harris stepped on a phantom tail when he went out for wood in the dark tonight. It yelped. I have put out tiny offers of food ever since our ancient back door cat died two weeks ago. I knew he was sharing with an opossum and with Cougar, the little stray, on occasion. But ever since he has been gone we have not seen either of them.

I put out the food at 9:00 P.M. When I check again at 10:00 P.M. it is usually cleaned up—someone has been accepting our offerings on a regular basis. And tonight it yelped and disappeared.

NOVEMBER 28 • *Night*

Last night's unseen, indignant howler was the opossum, Old Silver. My flashlight beam caught his startled eyes and wet, pink nose full on. He did not risk another encounter with a human's big shoe. The instant my light hit him, he left his prize, scuttled off the porch, and under the house. I heard him bumping along the furnace vents. This is one opossum that has found the good life.

But later when I check at 2:00 A.M., he has returned and has finished his scavenging in peace.

That wet nose of his should stand him in good stead as a nocturnal animal, particularly one that does not seem to see too well. The wetness collects scent molecules to help him find his way around in a dark world.

NOVEMBER 29 • *Night*

A lovely thin, wet snow fell all afternoon. It lights the darkness with a candlepower all its own. The night is as luminous as if earth hung in the bright shadow of a partial eclipse instead of in its own night shadow.

I can see all the limbs on the trees in the woods beyond the abandoned garden—fine white lines inked in frost.

A barred owl breaks the stillness. I see his darkness against the ghost-pale hill as he hunts between the whitened trees.

This is a good time for him. Any movement on that snowy ridge is visible as a radar blip on a blank screen. All of his mobbing daytime enemies are asleep, holed up for the duration. He owns this white night.

The silence is in his favor as well. His ears are well attuned to the slightest whisper of sound. They are hidden at the edges of his facial disc, offset for triangulation. If there is a sound, he will hear it. And know just where it comes from.

DECEMBER 1 • *Night*

After a week and more of never-ending, seamless gray skies and moisture-muffled sounds, which made us wonder if we were losing the full use of our senses, the clouds have finally lifted. Too late for our weatherman's promised forecast of a sunny first day of December. The moonlight is welcome nonetheless. I am not sure it is possible to forecast the weather in the volatile Midwest; Alberta clippers, warm Gulf Stream wetness mitigating the chill, cold gusts blowing off the Rockies—who knows what is going to happen next? Even with Doppler radar, which lets us know if a raindrop fell two counties over, it is still a surprise from day to day. From hour to hour, often enough!

Perhaps we are arrogant to assume we can predict the weather. We might as well guarantee the actions of the stock market or pinpoint the end of the world. It is no accident that we joke about Missouri's changeable weather. We can hazard a good guess, an educated guess, but we fool only ourselves if we imagine a Doppler omnipotence.

It cannot be an easy task, wherever you live—except, perhaps, in a hot desert summer. Moving weather fronts, slip-sliding jet streams, ping-pong highs and lows. Chinooks and Santa Anas, hurricanes, cyclones, tornadoes, temperature changes that come with the night and vary from county to county—I doff my hat to the weatherman. If he is right half the time, he is a seer; more than that, and he has attained prophet status.

It keeps life interesting. I enjoy the unpredictability, the endless surprise, Missouri or anywhere. I stand in the frozen moonlight and admire its lovely whitewash. It is twenty degrees at 10:00 P.M., and I do not even feel the cold.

This moonlit night is serendipity. As I watch, a single skein of snow geese—late migrators—unravels itself across that pale, almost-round moon face. I hear their high, wild cries and am inexplicably glad to be alive. If I had stood this afternoon to enjoy a sunny day—the sunny day that did not come—would I have walked in the moonlight tonight?

DECEMBER 2 • *Night*

After last night's twenty-degree low the soil under the rocks is still frosty. But a thin, red millipede slowly moves off when I disturb him in his hiding place. Perhaps I interrupted his final feast of the winter. These many-legged creatures are often active at night; this one may still be feeding on decayed leaves and plant roots.

A snail hibernates under the limestone rock, as cold as the soil and as still. It dug itself into the earth, closely fitted around the spiral shell like a rounded pebble. The soft body is pulled back into the helix and sealed tightly against the cold and against dehydration. Perhaps the dead air spaces sealed into abandoned chambers in the growing, calciferous shell will offer insulation through the long, silent months—escargot in cold storage.

DECEMBER 3 • *Night*

The moon hangs full over the hill behind the house, round as the head of a drum. It is the month of the Long Night Moon. The ancient Native American name calls up images of a people huddled in skin lodges, smoke rising from the hole at the top of the tipi and standing pale against the cold night sky. The moonlight catches the smoke and lights it, fluoresces the ghostly image. The Long Night Moon has spawned a child, wavering and changeable, sweetly aromatic.

The Old Farmer's Almanac for this year calls this moon the Cold

Moon, and it is that as well. The unaccustomed chill takes my breath away, and I wonder when I will adapt to the cold. Some winters I can stand to be out at twenty degrees without a jacket, but this cold cuts like a sharpened flint.

In the Southwest, bright Venus is chasing what is left of a clear, peach-colored glow beneath the rim of the world. If I were looking through a telescope, I could see that this first "star," the planet Venus, is not fully round; it goes through phases like the moon. A shadow changes its apparent shape from week to week, and I strain my eyes to catch its transformation.

DECEMBER 4 • *Night hike*

The icy gurgle of Rush Creek sounds colder still on a night hike. The sound carries across the hard ground as over open water. It was thirty degrees up by the intern's cabin where we started out. Here, in the creek's deep valley, the temperature drops as we sink into a river of cold air that falls back upon itself in nightly retreat. It seems to suck all the warmth from my body and carry it away downhill. The scent of frozen muck is clearly redolent, a memory of summer put by in ice.

As we walk, the frost forms sparkling on the grass. If we are still and hold our warm, melting breath, we can watch it form, molecule by molecule. I regret not bringing my pocket microscope. What small wonders am I missing?

We wake a cardinal as we pass. I hear its quick, inevitable complaint in the brush by the open trail. As we drop down into the bare woods, we startle up more sleeping songbirds, and they bucket away in all directions, banging through the trees. They do not see any better than I do in this darkness. I hear one ricochet off a branch with a thump and rattle.

We cross the creek on ice-fringed rocks, one by one, trying to keep our feet like slack-rope walkers on a greased cable. To spend the rest of the hike wet as well as cold sounds less than desirable even to the most hardy among us. I am wearing my old heavy loafers, though. I lose my footing and plunk into the icy shallows, but only the shoe is baptized. My foot is dry, if suddenly colder.

We search the bare branches for signs of life and see only Cassiopeia's open "W" hanging in the limbs of an ancient sycamore like a string of Christmas lights hung early in the old tree. We will try to call in the owls with the nature sanctuary's tape and big, state-of-the-art tape deck. Bill saw a barred owl here earlier; it seems the place to start. One night at the sanctuary the little screech owl came in to answer the taped summons. He could not resist the challenge when they played a rival screech owl's waver. The barred owl answered his own summons, that of hunger. He found the tiny ten-inch owl and summarily ate him before the horrified eyes of the night-hike crew. This time we are only trying barred owl calls. We did not want a repeat performance. It is one thing to know that screech owls are often prey to the bigger hunters, quite another to cater a small, feathered entrée.

We sit, an expectant audience of fourteen arrayed on wooden picnic benches, waiting for owls that decline our invitation. After the exertion of the hike, I am as warm inside my clothing as if I sat in my own living room instead of on a bench in below-freezing temperatures. Body heat is a wonderful invention, and my insulated underwear hugs it to me like a down comforter. A good thing, too; we wait in the cold for half an hour but the performance never begins. The owl is a no-show, as if he knew we did not plan to provide a meal this night.

DECEMBER 8 • *Night*

I go out to pay my respects to the warm, springlike night and find a lone, lined acrobatic ant in the cat food bowl. They have been in the house for weeks now, active nocturnally. But who would expect to find one still outdoors, still foraging? It seems sluggish. I blow on it, and it scarcely reacts.

They visit our bathroom lavatory for water during dry seasons at all times of the year. They make the foray from their nest in the crawl space under the house. The other night there was a winged reproductive among the worker ants.

They are so tiny, no more than an eighth of an inch, but usually smaller still. My insect books contradict one another. These selfsame ants, *Cremastogaster lineolata*, are either confined to Texas or may be found from Ontario to Florida. And in my Missouri bathroom.

DECEMBER 9 • *Daybreak*

After six days of overcast and drizzle and heavy, scudding clouds of an unremitting, tasteless, lumpy gray, I wait for dawn like a kid waits for Christmas morning. It will be clear today. It has been too long, even for me, and I like rain. I enjoy the drama of clouds. There was little enough drama in these; it was like wearing a bowl of cold oatmeal on your head.

Tatters of clouds in the east were a ruddy lavender against the darkness when I got up, then Payne's gray smudges against that growing light. Now the sky glows jewellike in contrast with the darker earth, and the bottoms of the clouds are painted coral.

We are going to see the migrating snow geese and the attendant bald eagles at Squaw Creek National Wildlife Refuge—and it will be a glorious day.

DECEMBER 9 • *Evening*

And so it was; nearly four hundred thousand geese filled the refuge with the sound of their voices and the thunder of beaten air through their wing primaries. My ears still drum with the avian percussion. We stood on the observation deck and watched as flock after flock circled and landed or rose in honking clouds only to circle and land again. Hundreds of muskrat lodges dotted the marsh, dark as peppercorns. A herd of deer watched us as calmly and as quietly as if they were equally taken by us. I could not watch them long enough.

And if our long ride home was marred by car trouble and anxiety and the thought that night would come home before we did, it was worth it. Now, safely back, I think only of the beauty of the day, and I wonder if the marsh is filled with the night sounds of those geese.

DECEMBER 11 • *Night*

At 9:00 P.M. I find Orion's diamond-studded belt in the southeastern sky, bright and clear against the velvet. The red star Betelgeuse sits on his shoulder like a jewel to clasp his cloak about him. Sirius, the Dog Star—Orion's faithful hunting companion—heels at his feet, well-behaved and trained by twenty billion years of practice.

My father raised pedigreed hounds. They were considered fine hunting animals, whippet thin and avid.

Bird dogs, they were, with hair-fine responses. But I liked best the little coonhounds and beagles that raised Cain in the night. On the farm we heard them tracking the hours, baying full-throated at the moon. I imagine Sirius to be one of these. My childhood beagle, the constant and dependable Rocky, would have followed me for twenty billion years as well, if he had had the chance.

The central stone in Orion's belt is fuzzy, indistinct through my binoculars. It is no star at all, but a bright nebula of space dust—the great nebula of Orion.

In the south there is a reddish glow. The far-off lights of Kansas City warm a low bank of clouds, raked and striated. By 11:00 P.M. the clouds have taken the sky hostage and eaten all the stars, one by one. It is odd; it still looks clear. The cloud cover is thin and dark as the night sky itself, not lit by the glow of the city or by the warm-colored sodium streetlights on Broadway. It is as if the night sky were suddenly wiped clean of stars and left waiting for a new equation to be put up on the blackboard. It would take a thousand Einsteins working in concert to do it.

DECEMBER 12 • *Sunset*

Coming home through the sunset from a book signing in Greenwood, I notice small groups and flocks and congregations of starlings, all heading west into the sun. I wondered why all the westering until I remembered the great winter roosting trees by the Missouri River—gigantic sycamores and cottonwoods that line the river banks near downtown Kansas City. The residual warmth from all the concrete and buildings must attract them.

The glacial loess hills were already blued with shadow as I came down into the river basin on Highway 291, but the orange sun lit the length of the river clear to Jackass Bend, tunneling down between the bluffs. The water glowed as orange as the sky, throwing the light back, changed and liquid. Then, as if turning off a light, the sun disappeared, leaving a tender mauve glow downriver, like a faded memory.

Later I watch through the icy, obscuring fog of my own breath as the Geminid meteors streak from the sky. Hard to believe—in this frigid night air—that all those glowing, fiery stars in the northeast, where the Geminids originate, are putting out thousands of degrees of heat like our own sun. The meteors themselves are burning up overhead in the friction of our atmosphere. I do not feel a thing but my own cold toes.

WINTER SOLSTICE

The Coming of the Light

WINTER IS A TIME OF SIMPLICITY AND OF SEARCH. The nights are endless, hours following reluctantly on one another's heels—cold, Siberian. The longest night of the year comes at the winter solstice, December 21. After that date, Michaelmas ushers in the light, moment by slow moment.

John Burroughs wrote that, in our climate, winter is the time when nature finally shuts up house and locks the door, and so it sometimes seems. In the absence of more easily achieved observations, weather itself often becomes the subject. The skies and their cold, glittering stars, the vagaries of temperature, the myriad permutations of winter water—frost, snow, sleet, freezing drizzle in a thousand forms. Snow squeals underfoot as if in pain when I walk its crusty surface at minus fifteen degrees. Icicles form like bars to incarcerate a stream for a season. Frost patterns on our windows and on each leaf and blade of grass seem incandescent in their night whiteness and glow like fox fire.

Played out against winter's subtle palette, sunrise and sunset are spectacular. I cannot look long enough at the fading of the day into night when the color of a June afternoon is contained in the setting of the sun: reds, oranges, maroons, lavender, and a piercing blue, even a transparent turquoise and jewellike green as the light disappears. I do not even notice the chill that invades my marrow as the evening stars appear, piercing that conflagration of color in the west. And the rising of the sun may be just as dramatic, as if running the film in reverse. I hear the crackle of the universe in that kaleidoscope stillness.

The nights seem deserted, save for the calling of owls. We have to look hard for signs of life. But life there is if we take the time to see it. I need only to bundle up to give myself the necessaries for night watching. As always, if I look, I am rewarded in the seeing. The invisible owls, whose calls I hear on the hill, are not disembodied ghosts. They become flesh and bone and feathers if I enter their territory—the night. And if they are active, it is with good reason. Prey animals are about as well. Meadow mice may make forays if the cold is not too deep. Rabbits venture out to feed, and the owls watch in silence.

Flying squirrels visit our birdfeeders at night. They are furtive as spies—good reason in itself to keep feeders well stocked. With luck, these tiny, huge-eyed foragers will not become prey to the resident owl population.

Owls are not the only nocturnal hunters in these dark hours. Foxes and coyotes also stalk the night, ears cocked to hear the messages broadcast beneath the snow. Stepping carefully, each foot placed catlike in the track ahead, the coyote moves like silence itself, listening intently. A stiff-legged pounce lands him squarely on a gopher that is burrowed half in the frozen earth, half in snow.

On one enchanted late-winter night, we spotted something that few witness these days: A lithe least weasel in winter mufti, white as the snow itself and intent on his mission, crossed the road in front of our car; he never even looked up. The light caught the longer guard hairs of his coat and turned them to silver; his grace was heart-stopping.

If I am willing to pay the price of cold extremities and a bit of discomfort, I find a wildness in these winter nights. And for me, winter comes not by the calendar or by the clock, but with the first, good, howling snowstorm. There is a turning in that event that alerts all our senses to the change in the season. We feel it. We hear it. It is winter.

DECEMBER 14 • *Dawn*

Daybreak has been whitewashed, and the snow is still falling. It is more pale blue-gray than white in the growing light. Hundreds of thousands of millions of flashes in tangled, untouching webs are airborne like the snow geese at Squaw Creek. But these pale shapes are wonderfully silent, settling on the earth like benediction. I catch one on my tongue like a communion wafer, and it is gone with the barest flicker of cold.

Only the jays are up and around so early—the jays and the new kittens and me.

DECEMBER 14 • *Night*

It snowed all day, the deepest in nine years here in Missouri—deep and damp and treacherous. My friend Marion, trying to get to her home up on the hill, went off the road in the dark, caught her car's axle on the curb at the corner, and has come to use my phone to call Roger. We all troop up the hill to kibbitz and to see if we can help as he jacks up the car, props it on concrete blocks and then tries to push it back into the road-way while Marian sits white faced behind the wheel. The police car's flashing light catches her paleness in blue, then red, then blue again, as it does the falling snow.

I had called the police to block the road at the bottom. No one can get by, or at least so it looks from where I sit. In fact, two daring souls from uphill squeaked by on the right angle and slide away down the hill, barely missing the police car. We hold our collective breath in the hope that one of them will not dislodge Marian's car prematurely and sent it off its precarious three-wheeled perch and onto Roger as he works the jack.

"Stand back!" he shouts, as he and a friend shove at the rear of the car to nudge it off the curb. "That jack could fly anywhere!" We stand back, and then some.

After three tries, and just as the tow truck comes wearily up the hill (poor Jack Orava's been at this since dawn), the car groans into the street and slides downhill with a long metallic sigh. And by the time I come back in the door at home, blowing and stamping like a draft horse, my jeans are ice, my shoulders are drifts, and my hair is white as my grand-mother's.

At midnight it is still snowing; there have been three more cars off the road at the corner. The garden has taken on an insulated stillness in the heavy snow, and the only sound is the grind and clank of the snow plow.

DECEMBER 15 • *Daybreak*

The snow has stopped. The sky is clear and golden against the blue earth.

The neighbor's house sports a gargoyle fringe of icicle teeth. The tree limbs in the woods wear Irish fishermen's sweaters of thick white wool that falls without a sound as the dawn wind rises.

Everything is changed, encased in a thick batting as if to protect it from break-age. Water—in all its winter forms—has put a spell on the forest. Strange, bulbous shapes loom where a stump or a fallen tree were. A small mound of brush in the understory is an Art Nouveau maze of elongated, graceful blue lozenges. In the yard, the barbecue and the old metal chairs, the bird feeder and the wood pile all wear pointed white gnome caps as if to a costume party. They all rented the same outfit by mistake.

Not a track disturbs the perfect whiteness. Not a dog, nor a cat, nor a bird, nor a 'possum has stirred this twenty-degree morning. Last night's footprints have disappeared beneath the blowing drifts. The Bigfoot tracks down the front walk, made by a small, bounding dog in the deep snow, have been smoothed by the wind's hand as well. Everything has a dreamlike roundness of contour, a morning drawn by Peter Max.

On the far hill, beyond the old-growth forest in the park, I can see steam beginning to rise from the houses as the townspeople take morning showers and fix breakfasts to fortify them against the long, hard commute or cold-morning chores. They look like geysers in Yellowstone's winter fastness, standing stark against the growing light.

Everything is done in shades of blue, except that glowing sky. Pale blue snow, deep blue-violet trees on the far hill, blue-gray icicles, periwinkle clouds—it is too lovely to last. The snow plow comes up the road again, clunking and belching up the hill, rearranging the perfect blue blanket into a rumpled coverlet, throwing it back roughly, getting us up for the day.

DECEMBER 19 • *Dawn*

My friend H. A. walked the path at Watkins Mill in the half-light and was startled by a strange, hollow barking from the woods. He stopped, thinking to hear a big dog bound through the snow-covered underbrush, but realized the sound was overhead instead. A great blue heron sailed just by him, pursued by a barred owl. It seems an impossible prey for the owl. A heron may be fifty-five inches long, not counting his legs, and a barred owl is twenty-four inches tops. It must have looked like songbirds mobbing an owl, so out of proportion are their relative sizes!

Such a strange occurrence could not go by without checking with the experts. I called in Joe Werner, urban biologist with the Missouri Conservation Department. His reaction was not so different from my own. "That's nuts!"

"Actually," he continued, "the heron may have blundered into the owl's nesting area or too close to the roost. Owls are extremely territorial and protective of their holdings, even if they've taken over a nest from another bird, like a redtail hawk, and rebuilt it."

We agreed that strange things indeed happen in the early morning hours before full light. H. A. appears to have been at the right place to see one of them.

It seems late for a heron to even be in the area. I do not expect to see one of these big birds hunting in the snow. But the lake is not yet frozen, competition is scarce, and perhaps the fish have not all headed for the warmer water in the depths of the lake. There must be a reason for all this oddness, but it proves—happily—one of my most treasured observations. We do not know everything. The world is delightfully mysterious, especially in these uncrowded hours.

DECEMBER 21 • *Night*

A hapless house mouse has met a grisly end in my attic on the first day of true winter. The solstice was at 10:28 A.M. this morning. It seems a bad time to die.

One of the traps I set this fall caught him by the neck. I see his pink, handlike paws, dainty toes like pink threads curled in death, and I wish I had remembered to spring the traps myself.

I put them in the attic when an influx of field mice threatened to turn the fiberglass insulation we had blown in last summer into an elaborate system of mouse caves. The smell of mouse permeated the attic and drifted down into the kitchen. I reluctantly protected my own territory from invasion.

But this is the first and only mouse we have caught in a long-forgotten trap. It makes me more determined to find a live trap at the hardware store. This killing is not for me.

DECEMBER 22 • *Night*

Fishing River is flint black, set like a stone in its snowy banks. In summer this same small feeder creek is clear, showing the pebbly bottom or the light brown of café au lait in flood. Each winter the water is inky. I could dip my pen in it to draw, or so it seems. Actually, it is as clear and cold as it will get. It is optical illusion accentuated by snow and midnight.

The water has yet to freeze solid. Even its chucklings seem cold. I hear the tinkle of ice forming at the edges, the soft whisper of moving slush in the little runoff that feeds into the creek in flood or wet seasons. There are flourishes of ice lace like Elizabethan ruffs at the throats of the limestone rocks upstream.

In the deep snow, it is easy to see where nocturnal animals have passed but not so easy to identify them. Their close-to-the-earth bodies have smudged their tracks; the unceasing wind obscures them further. Something has passed here in the night—many somethings—but their identity is mystery.

DECEMBER 23 • *Night*

I shiver in the cold. But it is not the cold that causes that involuntary shudder. It is a memory called up by this deep winter night. One year, when we still lived on the farm—just before Christmas, just after a snow—we heard a wild, quavering scream that echoed and bounced off the hills that bounded Shackleford Creek. It was like nothing I had heard before: not rabbit, caught by an owl; not human; not coyotes yodeling at the moon. It was—it may have been—the last bobcat in Ray County. *Lynx rufus* (*Lynx* refers to all lynxlike cats, *rufus* to the reddish body color) is rare in this part of Missouri, and becoming more so. Only scattered populations exist north of the Ozarks and this side of the Mississippi. Charles W. Schwartz's *Wild Mammals of Missouri* states there are a few animals in deep woods near the Missouri River. Our old farm was at the edge of old-growth forest only five miles from the river. That winter night I heard presettlement Missouri scream into the night, and I shivered.

DECEMBER 24 • *Night*

Insomnia on Christmas Eve—you would think I was a child waiting up for Saint Nicholas. Well, I have waited all night, and there is only the deep silence all around, except the tinkle of a neighbor's wind chime made sweeter by the night and the eerie sound of a coyote at the edge of town.

My wind sock turns and sways on the porch. The night has stolen its bright color and rendered it an ectoplasmic motion of wind and ripstop.

Margaret, the kitten, looks up at me big eyed, poised to pounce. I widen my eyes back at her and she flattens her ears and thinks better of the attack. It is a form of communication that never fails to elicit a response. In any man/animal confrontation, eyes have power. Never look an attacking dog—or certainly a bear—in the eye; it is interpreted as a challenge. Margaret thinks so, too, and measures my size against hers. No go. She and her sister, Coyote, are our Christmas presents to each other—a gift of life.

DECEMBER 26 • *Night, Morning*

The night is noisy with a thousand sustained whispers—the sounds of wrinkling cellophane and crackling pine-wood fires. A thin coat of ice dresses everything in sound.

Throughout much of the Midwest the ice storm has been ruinous. Here in northwest Missouri we are on the cusp. We have escaped heavy damage so far. In Springfield, south of us in the Ozarks region, electric lines are down, and traffic is snarled like dropped yarn. Accidents are epidemic. Thousands of homes are without electricity. In that part of the state, the National Guard has been called out to help homeowners and farmers by delivering food and kerosene heaters and electric generators to power milking machines. I hear whispers of all the activity in the crackling of the ice.

It is just above freezing here, not cold enough to turn the fine mist and drizzle into snow, but cold enough to solidify it on twigs and branches and electric lines. We watch it anxiously, wondering how bad it will get.

In the morning, a world turned treacherous with ice glistens in the growing light. An early rising squirrel makes his way to my feeder, feeling his way along his slippery route as carefully as a first-time skater on new ice. Birds slide out of control as they land on the feeder and find they have taken off again unexpectedly. It would be comical if I did not know how hungry they must be with their normal stores of weed seeds encapsulated in this hard, glittering shell.

We are grateful for the changes in our lives. For years, on ice-storm mornings like this, we drove the twenty-eight miles into Kansas City, taking up our lives in my shaking hands behind the wheel of the car. That twenty-eight miles seemed endless. We crawled by landmarks made oddly unfamiliar by the ice, beautiful but deadly as a coral snake. We passed car after car off the road, down embankments, upside down or simply sitting, disconsolate, beside the road. In the city, vehicles caromed off one another like bumper cars. Their drivers watched helplessly in rearview mirrors as a two-thousand-pound, out of control car hits from behind or slides sideways down an incline to crumple a fender.

One morning, when Harris had a ride, I took him out to the local discount store to meet his transportation. The store had a long, broad parking lot. In the ice it had become an ant lion's trap as cars lost control and slid helplessly down to crash into each other or into the building itself. We hit a small traffic island near the top, instead, and through the gloom Harris could just make out his ride at the bottom of the icy trap. He skated off downhill, and somehow they made it out through the lower exit.

I was terrified that another car would top that hill, lose control, and crush him on its way to the bottom. It was too dark to see well. He simply disappeared and never came back. At the bottom I could hear the long slide and the impact as yet another car came to meet rides or riders.

I was too shaky to do more than guide our car to a safer spot downhill—somehow—from the traffic island target and skate, flat-footed, over to the fast-food restaurant nearby. I nursed coffee until long after full light to build my courage for the attempt to escape. That morning, winter had taken captives. The restaurant was full. We were all prisoners of war to the need to make a living wage and somehow survive the ice storm.

Now as I look out on that glittering iciness and remember, it is with apprehension for my neighbors and friends still bound to the long road and with deep relief that I can go back inside, throw a log on the fire and read my morning paper in safety.

DECEMBER 28 · *Early*

The ice abated. It stayed warm enough in the northern part of the state to avoid the worst of it. The Ozarks are often plagued with ice storms and freezing rain when we get a pleasant, dry snow; we are just that far north. But this time we were in a strange inversion, a mitigating warmth. I cannot explain it, but I luxuriate in it—safe, this time.

We prepared, nonetheless. We brought firewood up on the porch to dry, stocked up on food, checked our supplies of batteries and kerosene for the lamps, laid in a stack of good reading. The wood stove and the luxurious warmth of the down comforter are survival in style in a hard winter. A hibernating woodchuck could not be more snug. I feel my own metabolism slow for the long cold. I gain weight. I crave carbohydrates. And it is not such a bad idea, either. Scientists who study seasonal depression triggered by fading sunlight have found that carbohydrates may alleviate a bit of the blues. I am all for it! A pot of beans and ham simmered all day on the wood stove served with fresh, hot corn bread cheer me beyond all reason.

DECEMBER 29 · *Midnight*

The long opaque string of cloudy days and cloudy nights is brightened, at last, with a shining crystal night. The sparkling, starry skies and a half-moon like a fire opal pendant are as welcome as sun.

I have come out to test the owl tapes' ability to attract a mate. The season of territorial dispute is almost here, and I am hoping to find a jealous—and vocal—landholder. But after trying the call of a great horned owl, a screech owl, and, at the last, the barred owl that usually brings some response, I give up. Only glittering silence—except for Prince, the Siberian husky chained on the hill. He, at least, is interested in my antics.

The snow has melted, but the ground underfoot still crackles oddly. The frost has heaved and buckled it into odd, monstrous earthworm castings of highs and lows. The popcorn crunch I hear is the miniature hills being trod back down to size.

DECEMBER 31 · *Night*

This night is as coolheaded and clear-eyed as a chess master. Venus hangs low in the western sky, so bright I thought it must be a plane. I brought out my binoculars to see. But no, it is the evening "star" with its steadfast, planetary light. Its luminosity fills the western sky and threatens to muscle in on the moon's territory.

I drive to the creek in the ten-degree cold to see what the last night of the year may bring. Venus is so brilliant; it hangs there alone, suspended upside down in the big pool by the bridge. No other star has the strength to show itself in the gently moving water. Venus points right at me, beckoning me down the creek.

What can I do? I go, stepping carefully in the darkness. The frost has heaved the bare ground here as well, and it is like walking on walnuts to get to the broad riffle downstream.

I am glad I follow the directive, though the going is not easy. With Venus hidden now behind Siloam Mountain's low flank, the other stars take their rightful places. They stud the sky like rhinestones and decorate the bare, etched branches of the trees on the hill.

Moonlight rides the riffle like fox fire, cold and slick and glittering, never quite swept away downstream, always moving. The moon is just past first quarter and growing. The almanac in the morning newspaper puts it at full on 3 January. It looks as if it will have to blow up like a balloon to meet its deadline.

I hear a whisper of sound. It is the thin, crisp ice that forms itself along the edges of the big pool. In the moonlight I see its crinkled surface moving slowly, riding the water, spreading outward from the banks, not yet locked into place. I find a dry, abandoned nut and chuck it into the fragile frill of ice to watch it break and rise along the spreading, concentric rings before reforming, reestablishing itself—resuming its inevitable sealing of the pool. By morning its work will be complete.

JANUARY 1 · *Dawn*

And so it was. This morning I drop a rock onto the ice and, instead of breaking through, it skitters off anxiously. Its sound is a hollowness, a strangeness.

JANUARY 1 · *Night*

The earth is pale, freeze-dried by the frigid temperatures. The ubiquitous puddle in the path's lowest point is decorated with the icy amoeba shapes of bubbles frozen in place. I test its surface gingerly, and it holds for a moment. Then a hollow crack sends me hopping back to *terra firma*, post haste.

The creekside pebbles and tiny, cryptic fossils are locked tightly in the iron earth, as if already compressed in aggregate rock, sealed for millennia instead of just a season.

I break a few larger pebbles free from the icy path, kicking them loose with my heel. Perhaps I can break the surface of the ice on the creek here where it just begins to move more quickly downstream. But instead, I break my own record for skipping stones. These never sink at all, but *shuush* clear to the other side and bounce back off the hard-frozen bank. Even where the ice looks thin and delicate as air, the rocks skip across the polished dance floor surface. Only where the riffle keeps water at a quick two-step do the rocks still plop through. Here, the icy edging is paper thin, striated with frost. When I chuck a stone through the ice at my feet, the frozen edge that reaches out into midstream copies concentric ripples at every small, stony peninsula, in multiples of twenty.

The long-dead skeletons of streamside plants smell sweet and fresh when I crush them between my stiff fingers. They prickle in my nose like frost. Nearby, dried, minty-looking calyxes yield up no scent at all.

Just by the creek there is another long puddle in a track excavated by ATVs. I trust my luck to smooth passage, half expecting the ice to ruck and buckle like a peat bog. It is as solid underfoot as the rocky limestone nearby.

Up the creek, where the water runs more swiftly, my meditation rock—inaccessible across the icy riffle—is frilled and lacy. A collar of fine Irish lace is tatted 'round its edge. Each rock wears a different pattern, as if in the lacemaker's own ancestral design—Battenburg, eyelet, knitted fringes of ice; angular fisherman's nets; snowflake mimics; delicate amoebic edgings—constellations of ice patterns. Everywhere I look there is a new design created by location and temperature and the molecules of freezing water. They glitter in my flashlight beam each in its turn.

It is cold and getting colder. I seem to feel the ice lace forming in my cells. My fingers are clumsy and suddenly pale in my light. It is time to head back.

JANUARY 2 • *5:47 P.M.*

The moon peers over the hill as round and as intense as an owl's eye. One night from full, and it looks as if it will burst with another day's growth, exploding and scattering bits of light like a supernova. How can it be that the bold light is merely a reflection and not incandescent of its own?

The sky is just ultramarine. Around the bowl's rim it is pale. The cobalt blue zodiacal light licked with copper in the west is a memory of a day that will not be back again. The evening "stars"—Jupiter, Venus—have been joined by real ones, two of them at least, pulsing in the sky. I watch to see what will next pierce that opaque blue overhead and render it slowly transparent in night's shadow cone, silver eyes multiplying in the darkness.

JANUARY 6 • *2:00 A.M.*

The clouds settled down around our ears sometime during the night. When I went to bed they were only a thin veil, softening the moon's razor edges. Through the oaks on the hill, the moon glowed like an illustration by N. C. Wyeth. I half expected to see a pirate stalk down the hill, knife clutched in his teeth, hair clubbed behind his neck, pantaloons blowing.

At 2:00 A.M. it is silent, frozen into a profound soundlessness. It is just zero, and nothing moves, not a leaf or branch, not a barred owl on the hunt, not a foraging opossum. I soak in the silence, spongelike, delighted, luxuriating, scarcely feeling the cold. "Silence is golden," someone has said, but not in this frozen darkness. It is silver gray and dark velvet, palpable in its overpowering presence. My ears ring with it.

Long before the dawn I see the clouds have frozen in place, caught short by the cold. Everything is coated with the icy shine—not just the frosty earth, not just the grass and fallen leaves, but to the very tops of the trees at the summit of Siloam Mountain. It is hard, hoary, a night-long accretion of hoarfrost formed as molecules of water froze to one another, melted and refroze. It is like paint dried on the windshield of my car and not like frost at all. The roads are treacherous, oil slick. Cars are ditched everywhere as people find that frost can be ice-storm slippery.

It reminds me of a morning four years ago when we drove into Kansas City over thick frost. We were nearly crawling, clawing our way along on studded snow tires. In the distance we saw a familiar but not quite familiar shape—an owl, but what kind? It was dark against the pale, frosted tree, slender, upright, with ears that stood at attention. A long-eared owl, uncommon in this part of Missouri (at least to my eyes) sat in a tree in the median strip watching this strange, crawling procession of vehicles. He must have felt we were harmless, trapped as we were in our cars. He neither flew nor moved. He just watched us impassively as we passed in review. We were so caught up in our journey, so caught up in our lives and jobs and responsibilities that we hardly noticed this ancient *Strigidae* in the bare branches of the elm.

JANUARY 7 · *Evening*

A meteorite drops like a stone to the horizon, silently shrieking in the deep silence and bright as Venus in the night sky. It was only just there, and it

is gone, ephemeral as the first flush of discovery. It is a bit late—the Quaternids appear from 1 January to 4 January and are said to peak on 3 January. Said to, at any rate. I saw nothing during the assigned time, but now this bright speck of space debris rockets down toward the horizon in the southeast, lost, too, from its appointed northern-horizon locus.

MIDWINTER

The Nights Shorten, the Cold Strengthens

It IS AN ODDITY OF NATURE that as the dark hours lose ground and the daylight advances each day, winter makes its strongest assault. We are caught in the tension between two forces; the mercury drops, half convincing us it will never be warm again, but the slow victory of the light tells us the plain truth. This may be midwinter, but its power is already broken.

I hold tight to that talisman. Day by day the second hand of my watch points unmistakably to a few more moments of light.

Nights are less accessible than they were before, less bearable. We have no natural defenses against the insistent chill and must create our own as add-ons. We have neither fur nor feathers to keep us from the cold. We make no natural antifreeze in our bloodstream like many of nature's pragmatic alchemists. We will suffer from hypothermia or frostbite or worse, if we do not take proper precautions. The body loses up to 80 percent of its life-sustaining heat from an uncovered head as warmth wicks upward following the path of least resistance. We become a chimney for the venting of our own body heat. And like a furnace that loses too much heat up the stack, that is not good. Energy is burned to no good use.

But given the advances in winter gear and the timeless comfort of wool, we may still make brief forays into night. By monitoring our own condition, watching for early-warning signs of frostbite or overchilling, we can safely explore the night hours.

And there is always something to see. True, the compost heap is still now, deserted as an ancient Indian cliff dwelling. There are no sweet-scented wildflowers sending out their invitations to insect pollinators. If there were, those creatures are not here to receive them. The midnight skies are nearly deserted. But owls still hunt those thin corridors and, if we are lucky, we will spot one on his way. Mammals track the pale blank page of a snowy night and leave their stories written in Gothic bold if we take the time to read them. I can find fox and coyote, Eastern cottontail and mink if I look closely. With practice and the sort of patience it takes to learn computerese, I can read their cryptic stories. They are as powerful and as poignant as a Wendell Berry novel.

Often, here in the Midwest, winter makes an abrupt about-face. January thaw whistles in on warm Chinook winds melting our defenses along with the snow and filling our ears with sweet blandishments. The night smells of spring. It lies in our faces. I almost buy the scam. And although I know the thaw will pass, I make the most of these warm winter hours. Long walks become the order of the night, for me and for the nocturnal creatures that make hay in this balmy bounty. The raccoons and I explore like children and sense instinctively that it is still winter's cold, hard, dead center. It *is* winter, after all, for all the sweet lies and whispered promises. We are prepared for the inevitable turnaround.

Meanwhile, many animals are making preparations of their own, laying plans for the future. It is mating time for many of the night's creatures. Owls are breeding and watching over nest eggs of their own, their hedge against tomorrow. Foxes sing to their mates and promise territory rich with prey. Deer may already have mated and have begun their long wait for spring. Monogamous beavers, snug in their lodges, are expecting young. It is midwinter but pregnant with spring.

JANUARY 9 • *Night*

Great, fat snowflakes drift and tumble slowly from an apparently clear sky. They glitter against the darkness. The moon is hung large and hazy in the west, its edges melting, freezing, flaking away to become the falling snow. A few Spartan stars pierce the haze, as if the rest had lost their grip on the firmament and were falling, helpless and dreamlike, to earth.

These are flat, delicate dendrites falling together in snowy clumps. When they hit my sleeve, I can study their endlessly varied shapes. Hexagonal—and infinitesimal—water molecules have decreed this six-sided shape, this geometric order in the midst of natural chaos. The sheer numbers of molecules that make each crystalline flake account for their individuality. How could they be the same with the astronomical number of possible combinations of forms? But in November of 1986, two apparently identical flakes were photographed by scientists; another mercurial fact has lost its hold in the immutable firmament and tumbles to earth like snow.

The thin cloud cover—no more than a wisp of frozen vapor—is falling bit by bit, silently, into the night. When it has exhausted itself, used itself up, the snow will stop, and the sky will be as full of stars as ever. The earth glows phosphorescent with the promise, flashing like Saint Elmo's fire.

JANUARY 10 • *Evening*

I step out into the last of the light to add fuel to the frozen compost heap and to admire the cold, greenish glow of the sky against the darkened earth. As I turn to go back into warmth and supper smells, I see from the corner of my eye three knots in the bare, etched branches of the slippery elm. There is last summer's abandoned robin's nest. It is haunted, perhaps by the black snake's shade; the tangle of branches and leaves where the near-tornado decapitated the tallest branch; and now by a new darkness with a form I know, a welcome smallness in the tree. It is the screech owl, picked out against sky glow. His ears are up as if in caricature of listening, but he hears me well enough. I see that small head swivel on stubby shoulders, following the snow crunch of my footsteps. His golden eyes are invisible in the black silhouette. I can only just discern the lighter belly and the claws clutched over a black limb.

I whistle a sorry imitation of owl calls, but it is no go. My repeated tries only serve to freeze my pucker in place. It is near zero, and I came out without a coat, on an errand only and not a bird-watching jaunt. Still there is something in that small predatory form that holds me as securely in his grasp as if I were a meadow vole. I can no more move than fly to join him.

He flies—but only to the next tree. Perhaps he is considering my whistled invitation, my quavering trill—considering, but not consenting to answer. I have heard him often enough to whet my appetite for more. Although he was named for the European screech owl, this is pure slander. His sweet, descending trill, repeated usually twice and then followed by a rich contralto warble, is night music.

Suddenly, I am *determined* to hear that sweet quaver. I want to hear what he has to say, to consider his opinion, to get an owlish tongue-lashing for my sorry attempts at dialogue. I hop inside for my owl tapes and my coat.

It takes long minutes to find the tape, more to find the band with screech owls. The boom of a great horned owl would only serve to drive him off, and who could blame him. Screech owls are excellent prey for their larger cousins—tasty bits of protein and warm blood.

No wonder the smaller, eight-inch owls have learned the art of ventriloquism. They have perfected the art through evolution and need. This little screecher can adjust the muscles in his throat to allow more or less air through. You literally cannot tell where the sound is coming from.

Over and over I try the taped owl calls. I can see him in his new perch by the edge of the abandoned garden. But he is in no mood to talk. He considers my invitation and politely declines. He shows me his tail feathers as he disappears into the woods on soft-fringed, silent wings.

JANUARY 12 • *10:00 P.M.*

Coming home after a parks board meeting I see moving lights in the beam of my headlights. Some animal at the edge of the woods looks toward me, then away, then back again. The lights are low to the ground and glow reddish in the unbroken dark like two moving, lighted signal lanterns.

It is only Cougar, the small stray. The angle of the light made her eyes glow red rather than the normal cat's-eye green I am accustomed to. When my headlights, beams struck the membrane at the back of her choroid or retina, the *tapetum lucidum* reflected back at me. Literally a "bright carpet," this cell layer lives up to its name. The moving flashes are as bright as if the little cat had held up twin mirrors and sent me a semaphore message—of hunger, in this case. When she recognizes my car, she comes running!

Cats, dogs, deer, opossums, weasels, foxes all send back these flashes of bright light to us. We have the same (if diminished) ability. If you have ever seen a picture of someone taken with an inexpensive flash camera—one where the flash is mounted too close to the lens—you may have seen this same demonic glow reflected from human eyes. Our "bright carpet" is not as densely woven as mammals who see more efficiently at night. We have lost much of our nocturnal ability, and the rods and cones in our eyes that give us the ability to collect light and discern color are only a remnant of what we once had.

With 120 million photoreceptors in each eye, it would seem we were still well equipped to deal with the business of seeing, of translating the light we receive into electrical impulses that our brains then read as images and objects. We read and understand with only nanoseconds between. In night's low light, cones recede and rods advance—a *moving* carpet programmed to function as needed; the rods are more light sensitive. We see less color but images are enhanced. If we give our eyes a chance to adapt to the night (leave the flashlight at home and trust our own equipment), we are amazed at how much we can actually see.

Our eyes are exquisitely designed to respond to our environment. Shine a light in my eyes, and the pupil reacts instantly by contracting to a near pinpoint. In low light and at night, my pupil dilates to receive as much light—as much information—as possible. If I leave my flashlight behind on these nocturnal investigations, I can see far more than just those objects impaled by the beam. My field of vision is enhanced, though there is much less color and somewhat less clarity..

Still, our domestic felines—and all nocturnal mammals—are far better equipped for night sight. Cougar outstrips me with an additional ten *million* photoreceptors.

JANUARY 13 · *Night*

Cougar has brought an amorous male with her. She is at the beginning of her heat cycle, giving out the signals that tell the resident males she is in estrus, but not yet ready to be mounted; not by any stretch of the imagination. She must be wooed, convinced of her suitor's ability as a mate, and that will not happen until she has a circle of males to choose from. To the victor, in this case, goes the spoiled—Cougar is a pampered young flirt.

The males are extremely cautious as they approach her; those small claws and teeth inflict a lot of damage. Now, they gather, one by one, and consider their options.

Her cycle reminds me it is time for mating for many of the night's inhabitants. On the hill, the male owl will be bringing small prey to offer his female, as if to show her that not only is he a fine provider of small furry things but that the territory he has chosen has plenty of available prey—a good neighborhood with plenty of shopping and good schools for teaching the young to hunt.

Deer may already have mated, and the females' long wait has begun. In Missouri, however, breeding season can last until mid-

February. I find the shed antlers of bucks, if I am lucky and beat small, gnawing animals to them. They are loosened after rut by the resorption of bone at the base. This may be the result of a decrease in testosterone, the male hormone, but nutrition is also a factor. A well-fed buck in good condition retains his antlers longer.

In another week or so, the resident population of year-old opossums will begin their first breeding season. With a gestation period of only thirteen days, it is little wonder the young must find their way by instinct alone to their mother's pouch, or die. At birth these marsupials are earless and eyeless—little more than fetuses at a half inch long. The opossum's pouch is sometimes called her second womb. The tiny, half-formed young each find a nipple, attach themselves, and stay until they are more fully developed, eating and growing around the clock.

In years past, we have heard the sounds of mating in our basement. But this year we seem only to have Old Silver in residence. It is an on-again, off-again affair. He comes when he will.

If the weather is mild—during the January thaw, perhaps—little brown bats may mate. They've bred already, in the fall before hibernation; but the warming weather may put them in breeding condition again as they become more active.

Down by the creek, night-active beavers begin looking for mates. Adults often mate for life; monogamy among the animals is not that uncommon.

The barking of foxes tells me their breeding season has begun. Foxes mate from late December to March, but individual females have a very short heat period—only two to four days a year. I listen closely to the pair that lives on the hill; their assignation is tonight.

These early breeders insure, for the most part, that the young will reach maturity at the optimum time, given their particular gestation periods, maturation needs and prey cycles. There is rhyme and reason here, and Cougar and her circle of suitors are not alone.

JANUARY 15 • *Predawn*

A balmy daybreak makes me look involuntarily for signs of spring. It is the January thaw, and the air is scented with rumors of life. It is too soon for crocuses and snowdrops, I know. Their emergence is keyed to the lengthening of days and not this fickle false spring. But overhead in the growing light I can see the granular buds of the old Norway maple next door beginning to swell. They are already a valuable food source in these cold hard months. Squirrels and birds find them to their liking. It must be a bit like eating dry cereal. The buds are too small and tight in January to contain much moisture and, if they did, it would freeze. They are about as succulent as granola at this point.

JANUARY 16 · *Sunset*

A walk beside the river makes me wish I could manufacture glycopeptides in my bloodstream like certain arctic fish. This natural antifreeze allows the fish to flourish in water below freezing. It felt warm enough to forego gloves and hat when I left the house; by the time I reach the bridge I am chilled through.

I can see tiny new bud scales of elms etched clearly against the light and the larger bud clusters of maples. The oaks and walnuts are keeping thoughts of spring to themselves. They are still bare and dead looking. The pale sycamores—the only visible and entire tree forms countering that darkness—still cling to their seed balls like ornaments hung too long on the Christmas tree.

The creek is liquid onyx, reflecting nothing of the luminous sky behind Siloam Mountain. It is channeled between two graceful cuffs of white lace—the remainder of the prethaw ice that silenced the little creek, bank to bank, except in the quick, rocky shallows.

JANUARY 18 · *Night*

I hear it coming from a long way off. The night is soundless, still, a well of darkness. There are no stars, only unbroken clouds stained that peculiar ruddy hue from the sodium vapor lights downtown.

I hear the wind start up far away in the vacuum of sound, a muffled roar that sounds at first as if it is in my blood. But naked limbs deep in the woods move and groan. Then the sound comes closer and closer until the tree just overhead tosses, agitated. For a moment it is as loud as a full-leafed summer storm and then, as quickly as it came, it passes on, ruffling feathers half a county away.

In the chill it is hard to find signs of life. The compost heap is deserted. I find nothing at all, not even with my pocket microscope, but it is only thirty power. For a minute, digging at the base of the heap, I think I have found something, a particularly hardy, threadlike nematode, a sightless worm in miniature. But it is only a filament of something green and man-made. There is no life about it.

Looking under stones, I see the tracks of worms and beetles in the cold, damp earth and holes like tiny caves leading deep into the soil, but there is only the lone snail still sealed in darkness. He will not move until spring rains and warm weather.

What makes us long for signs of life these unending winter nights? Why do we feel alone, abandoned, bereft in a frozen universe? Even though I know that seeds keep their tiny packages of life safe until the spring, even though I can see the swelling bulbs of wild ramp in the woods that tell me that spring is contained within those primitive layers, even though maple buds swell and redden in the cold, I still need signs of life more closely related to my own to take the edge off a kind of existential loneliness. A bug would do it, or a snail on the move. Tonight there is nothing but the wind.

JANUARY 20 • *Evening*

The clouds are so laden with moisture that they hang down around my shoulders and slap against my face like wet spider webs. I take a quick

walk in the last of the day as the weak gray light slides off into a crack in the west.

I walk around the limestone rim of the old section of town and look down on the horizontal smoke that fills the valley like a bowl.

Up here, I am literally in the trees, eye level with last summer's nests and the excavations of woodpeckers. The wintering birds have all gone to roost. Among the bare branches I can find no sign of starling or jay, chickadee or titmouse or cardinal. No pigeon huddles on a limb; no flicker whirs his odd metallic cry at me. They have all gone. Night is falling, and the cold fills up the valley, claiming new territory on the hills. As I walk chin up and searching, I think I have found a bird at last. But it is only an oak leaf clinging stubbornly to its twig.

I know where the starlings have gone. I have seen them huddled cheek by feathered jowl along the Missouri River like black leaves on the pale branches of the cottonwoods. Crows have communal roosts as well; one south of town attracts large numbers of them. I watch them heading home at night, commuting by twos and threes to the suburbs.

The other birds may huddle for warmth as well. Though not generally flocking birds, many of the small passerines take advantage of shared body warmth on cold winter nights, bundling together like Puritans in a protected spot, presumably without an impure thought amongst them.

Still others use last summer's nests for a winter roost or build a separate "dormitory nest" nearby for just that purpose. That way they can still remain in home territory.

Many birds make use of nest cavities drilled by woodpeckers and flickers or find natural cavities in trees. They share space for the most practical of reasons. A few may even spend the long winter nights in our bird houses. No wonder we do not see them perching, exposed, on bare branches; they have more sense than that.

JANUARY 21 • *Predawn*

A light snow during the night has sketched everything in pale blue—the trees, the fence, Saint Francis in the herb garden. There was no wind to disturb the gentle falling; each flake settled where it struck first. The reflective phosphorescence makes it seem lighter at this hour than it normally is.

A male cardinal in full mufti must have thought so, too; he is already at my feeder. It is still dark enough that his red feathers look charcoal maroon, his flame damped to embers. A diet rich in carbohydrates helps sustain life through these long, cold nights. He seems to appreciate my offerings of birdseed mixed with cracked corn. The thermometer hovers around zero degrees. I am glad I remembered to fill the feeder yesterday.

JANUARY 23 • *Early*

Starlings huddle for warmth around our neighbor's chimney, tails all turned in to the rising heat, heads out to watch for come what may. These are up and about early. Wherever their roost is—and it may be thirty miles away—they made good time to get back here by daybreak.

At normal speed, most birds can be clocked at twenty to fifty miles per hour. Starlings, with their short, kitelike wings, should be capable of making the trip from the river roosts in a half an hour or so. They have nothing on the white-throated swift, though. This bird earns its name. Its speed has been estimated at two hundred miles per hour.

JANUARY 23 • *Late*

A noisy winter wind whistles up an audible wraith of summer. Everywhere the creak and complaint of limb on limb, of wooden gate against its hinge mimic the sounds of a summer night. There is a sound of crickets and katydids in the trees, but it is only the stone-cold wind, gusting to forty miles per hour. The chimeral sound of false summer warms the night—only for a moment.

JANUARY 25 • *Predawn*

The frost has drawn delicate etched-glass designs on my windows. In the growing light they are first pale blue, then sparkling white, then, as the sun fully rises, they blaze for a instant before they slowly begin to melt in on themselves along the edges in the imperceptible heat of an eight-degree morning.

This fugitive mycelium of frost marks the passage of warmth and moisture from my house into the night air. It is the breath of the building itself. It gathers along the bottoms of the windows where there is the least turbulence and where heavy, moisture-laden, colder air collects, molecule by molecule. Like snowflakes, these lovely patterns are geometrical, following the immutable laws of freezing water, and they are formed by water melting and recrystallizing over and over through the night.

They have followed the paths blazed by filaments of last summer's spider webs, which cling to the inside of the storm windows at the upper edges of the lacy designs. Their random delicacy changes into glittering linear designs like Mondrian gone as mad as Van Gogh.

Like an electron microscope, frost enlarges details we cannot begin to notice with our unaided eye. Leaves of dead weeds and cattails by the creek are fringed with nearly invisible hairs that wave like cilia in the breeze. They are delineated and enlarged by the night's frost until they claim our attention at last. The tiny hairs on gill-over-the-ground's scalloped leaves are each beaded with frost opals. Who would have noticed such details without frost's accretions?

JANUARY 26 • *Night*

The Dipper stands straight up on its handle in winter position in the sky. If it *could* hold water, it would only freeze. At five degrees, everything is

frozen. The ground underfoot is granite. My breath freezes on my glasses, alternately clearing and fogging as my lungs draw in the cold air and then expel warmth. Even in the dark, prismatic colors tint the world in pastel washes. The cold moon is rose and blue and back again to rose. My breath makes midnight glories of its light.

It is so cold that to breathe is to get a headache. The lungs rebel; they want no part of this frigid cold. My blood seems to scrape through protesting veins in a scarlet crystal slush: ice.

My down-filled comforter will feel good tonight. It is old and flaccid, but the pure white down feathers of ducks and geese that fill it help hold my body heat in against the cool bedroom air. It did the same for the birds who wore it originally. Each small, soft feather is made up of delicate, blowy barbs and barbules that trap the warm air and hold it fast in warm embrace. These tiny down feathers lack vanes altogether—the easily regained flat surfaces that make up the body of what we normally think of as a feather. Birds groom their feathers by pulling the vanes back into place. Down feathers have no need for this neat—and neatening—trick. They serve the purposes of insulation instead.

The best European comforters are still called "eiderdowns," since their insulation is taken from the Common Eider. This duck has abundant down feathers at her breast; as she plucks them to line her nest they are harvested by down pickers, with no apparent harm either to the female eider or to her offspring.

My own comforter was an inexpensive job. Small feathers migrate through the cover at night and, from that slow migration, I can tell that many of them are not down at all, but semiplume feathers or even body or contour feathers with their bits of down at the base of the rachis, the part of the feather we call the quill. Some mornings it looks as if a snow flurry fell over my bed in the night, and I pick feathers like an eider harvester.

JANUARY 29 · *Dawn*

The warm, languid breath of a Chinook wind has softened the cold angularity of a winter night and melted its contours until the dawn is soft as spring. January thaw is welcome whenever it comes. After these last marrow-chilling nights it is a most honored visitor. This month we have been doubly blessed—thaw came twice.

The dawn chorus is heavy on percussion with the blue jays' raucous, metallic *jay-jay* providing snare drum. Starlings polish their repertoire with a semimusical *queeee-oooo* dominating. This early in the morning—in the year—the cardinals seem only percussive. Their sharp *chip, chip, chip* syncopates the warm-up. They are not singing their exultant *pretty, pretty, pretty*.

I would swear that a common yellow-throat adds his *witchety, witchety, witchety, witch* to the chorus, but it is awfully early in the year for him. I wish I were more of a birder—what can it be?

A closer look reveals the singer. He is sparrow-sized with an eye stripe like a slash. A Carolina wren winters over here and sings a sweet, quick song, redolent of warmth.

JANUARY 29 · *Midnight*

The stars wheel in the sky like moths. They circle slowly around the North Star, seeming to arrow straight ahead through the darkness. Why don't I hear their soft *shuushing* through the sky—the air that beats through their wings? A train whistle enters the spaces between the stars and tangles itself in the unseen webs of limitless orbits. The rumble of the iron wheels are the iron and ice of the planets, the sound of comet tails against the silence, the ribald antic union of the finite with the infinite.

JANUARY 30 · *Night*

The lovely strange Chinook that made these January nights more like June has brought oddities we do not expect to see in deep winter. Night gnats—two, three of them—circle the porch lights like tiny moths, fasting in the absence of edibles. They are like moving bits of light against the darkness. Unlike summer's gnats that want to explore the warm, damp caves of nasal passages like insect spelunkers and admire their own reflections in my eyes, these have no interest in me whatsoever.

And later, the day-long clouds that hung like a warm mist erupt into sound and fury. The encroaching cold front demands territory from the gentle warmth and finds that warmth unwilling to give ground—and surprisingly vocal about it. A summer storm lasts throughout the long winter night with neon explosions of aerial electricity jarring us from our beds.

By dawn the warmth is vanquished, and winter has returned, but it was no easy-won battle. We bear the scars of fatigue from our noisy, sleepless night.

JANUARY 31 · *Night*

The temperature continues to drop until Janus' month reclaims its birthright—the January thaw is over. A noisy sleetfall fills the night with invisible sound. I cannot see the falling. I do not see it strike and bounce like miniscule, frozen BBs, but the relentless rustle and whisper is everywhere in the trees.

I do not see the sleet fall, but I feel it stinging against my face and on my bare, uplifted palms. It tastes as icy and as pure as snow—as pure as the clean white colorless color of snow. It is hard to believe that this childhood pleasure now holds its threat of danger. Ice pellets form around nodules of pure pollution. Acid rain falls in winter as a poisonous snow, a tainted sleet. At the Martha Lafite Thompson Nature Sanctuary in nearby Liberty, Missouri, a measuring device has been set up in cooperation with the Audubon Society to read the pH of falling precipitation, in whatever form it comes. Its acidity has been measured at pH 4.5, just slightly less acid than a cola drink; acidic enough to kill fish eggs; acidic enough that snails and tadpoles, bass and trout begin to die. It is not a problem of Canada or of the industrial Eastern states any more. We cannot pretend it does not affect us. We cannot "let someone else handle it." It is everyone's problem.

HINTS OF SPRING

Indications of Things to Come

LIKE WOOL SOCKS IN THE WASH, night has begun to shrink in on itself. Sunset comes later each night, the changeable dawn earlier. The sweet lies told by a January thaw melt slowly into fact. We can believe what we see, trust what we feel. No matter what the groundhog tells us on 2 February, the earth has its own timetable, and changes have been set in motion.

The plain fact of a minus-ten-degree night is only circumstantial evidence. There is an airtight case for spring. The first tender daggers of tiny, ground-hugging crocus pierce the chilly soil, not only pierce it but have the cheerful audacity to bloom. Mine wear miniature dunce caps of snow, but I no longer trust the sworn testimony of crystalline water. The crocuses know better; their empirical evidence is indisputable. No matter that February's moon is called the Snow Moon, no matter that snow itself squeals underfoot in a below-zero night as if we injured it with our passing. We believe what we want to believe. Spring is on its way, and none too soon.

And still this is the best time to observe the winter, the last of the beast. Its hold may be weakening, but there are nights during which I can believe it immutable. In the stop-and-go progress toward equinox, winter seems to hold the stronger cards. We may have our coldest night in this changeable month—our deepest snow, our most deadly ice storm. Blizzards are common occurrences, as if winter meant not to give up, not without a good scrap.

I am restless in February. I want a change. I see the clues everywhere. I listen to the sly insinuations. I hear the whispered promise of spring on the freshening breeze, and I want *action*. Winter's worn out its welcome, and I am bored with its long stay.

It is little wonder. February is a tease. I have never had much patience with this particular trait, this fickleness, this unreliable, unstable demeanor. February makes its promises, offers us a taste, lets us see plain evidence before our eyes, then tears spring from our grasp and laughs in our faces.

For proof and reassurance, I probe the night for signs like a druid seer. I hope to find them, concrete and visible, one fine morning. I count the transmutations on my fingers and on the abacus of change that calms my impatient mind. I repeat them to myself in the dark, a litany of metamorphosis, winter into spring.

Let me see. There are buds on the trees that threaten to pop; they glow with new sap as if lit from within. Moths return to streetlights. Jonquils and tulips seem impatient to join the grasslike crocus—I find their pale yellow spears lining the walk. In the woods, harbinger-of-spring shines like fallen stars against the dark of the forest floor.

Early birds stage a return. The reunion is tense as family members meet and compare notes on the virtues of staying behind to hold down the avian fort or leaving winter's difficulties behind and flying off to Rio. And sometimes the premature returnees taste bitter cold and have cause to regret their impulsive decision. Fickle February cannot help but play its practical jokes. We have to learn to laugh.

It can be done. Because that plain evidence is there to see, we can view February's flightiness with charity. I muster up compassion to endure winter's last gasp. I gather the vestiges of my near-spent patience. Spring *will* come. It always has.

FEBRUARY 2 • *Dawn*

If the overcast skies are any indication, dawn will find the groundhog snug and hibernating still in his den and not about to come out to predict the end of winter for a bunch of addled humans. Daybreak is as dim as a total eclipse, as dim as anyone who seriously believes the groundhog has something to tell us.

Groundhog Day has its roots in the Medieval English celebration of Candlemas, a day commemorating the presentation of Jesus in the temple. Altar candles are blessed on this day. As an old rhyme has it:

> *If Candlemas be fair and bright,*
> *Come, winter, have another flight.*
> *If Candlemas brings cloud and rain,*
> *Go winter and come not again.*

Just how we got from Jesus in the temple two thousand years ago to a gnawing mammal prognosticating on the end of cold weather, I cannot imagine. And why his shadow foretells the change is an even further stretch. The evolution of *myths*, at least, seems to work in fast forward, and there is a missing link there somewhere.

In any case, it is all a bit academic. We will have six more weeks of winter by the calendar, and that is for sure. From 2 February to the official vernal equinox is just six weeks. Groundhog or no, Candlemas or no.

But I have lit a small candle to shine through this grim, gray morning. It is cheery and scented and lifts the heart.

FEBRUARY 3 • *6:30 P.M.*

The snow clings to the last of the day like a great mirror. The earth, normally darkened by this time of a winter's evening, is pale and reflective. The shapes of feral dogs move against the lightness on the far hill. Small nocturnal animals make targets of themselves for the resident owls.

I heard a barn owl on the hill last night. These rare birds with the quizzical, heart-shaped faces are becoming rarer still as we tear down the old barns that offered perfect nest sites among their vaulted rafters. Dead trees are removed too rapidly to provide nest holes, in town, at least. My ramshackle garage might tempt a broody owl, close as it is to the edge of the woods, but even that must go. Built sometime in the 1920s, it survived (just barely) the 1976 tornado that skipped airborne through town. It is about to fall, and the chance of its injuring a curious child is just too great. No barn owls will find a home here.

The eighteen-inch owls are seldom seen in northern Missouri these days, but I heard an avian impersonator on the hill last night, a barn owl holding forth with—as the *Audubon Society Field Guide* says—"rapid, gracklelike clicks, hissing notes, screams, guttural grunts, and bill-snapping."

But this is scarcely the rarest owl in the neighborhood. A friend spotted a snowy owl near Resurrection Cemetery last week. This big white bird with bittersweet chocolate barring is an erratic from the far north, or to use the more precise ornithological term, an irruption. Perhaps game is scarce up north. During one irruption of snowies blown down from the Arctic with a Siberian express, the desperately hungry owls attacked fur hats, raccoon tails on the antennas of cars, even leather gloves. Imagine the consternation of a glove wearer as a big, starving snowy owl, with its fifty-five-inch wingspan tried to strip the sorry bit of nutritive value right off his hand.

It was commonly supposed that snowies only came south when the periodic reduction in lemming populations forced them to seek employment elsewhere. Lemmings have a habit of banding together to migrate, drowning by the thousands as they reach the sea and run out of any place to go. Every four to seven years, when local populations explode in a lemming parody of planet earth, these animals head for open country, never meaning to commit mass suicide in the nearest body of water, of course, but only falling to their deaths with the crush of the crowd behind them. When they do, the snowy owls miss their prey greatly and head out themselves.

But as Jonathan Maslow notes in his excellent book, *The Owl Papers*, that is not the only reason for snowy owl incursions. They have returned to the same place below the Canadian border for three years in a row to feed on a burgeoning population of Texas blacktail jackrabbits, creating, as Maslow points out, a most curious situation: arctic owls traveling to New York to find Texas jackrabbits escaped from a crate and multiplying like—well—like rabbits. They know a good thing when they see it; jackrabbits are considerably meatier than lemmings.

Joe Werner, urban biologist for the Missouri Department of Conservation, says that our arctic visitor is more likely an immigrant than a real tourist. This far south, he will stay to live out his life in a foreign land. Bird-watchers, naturalists, and ornithologists have made the pilgrimage to Clay County to see this anomaly. To call such an incursion into Missouri rare is to understate the case.

FEBRUARY 4 • *11:00 P.M.*

The Snow Moon looks small, chill, shrunken in on itself for warmth. Its light seems constricted, too. Through the slight haze, the light is diffused, dissipated into nothingness. The snow itself puts out more light.

It takes the moonlight and the lights from our houses and street lights and cars and throws it back in the face of this weak moon in derision.

FEBRUARY 5 • *Night*

There are stories told in the night, secrets betrayed, gossip writ large for all to see on the blank slate of last night's unmarked snow. This morning that virginal white is stitched with tracks, following the moving needle of their makers.

The red fox has made its dainty, careful way along the river, one foot following the other in single file. The luxuriant tail has softened the tracks as it flags out behind the small, nocturnal animal.

The feral dogs that track the hill with their braided trails have wandered the night, as well, keeping themselves moving against the cold. I imagine their breath in puffs of dog-scented steam, frozen on their muzzles at minus five degrees.

A cat has made its way down to the icy creek to sit beside the riffle held fast in winter's cold epoxy. But now, he has discovered a square foot of open water where the riffle runs quickest over the rocks. He has found a drink, if nothing more. I see the mark of his haunches beside the water. Then the little flowerlike tracks turn and investigate the interesting scents along the creek. The cat is a tom. He has marked his territory with scratches on a small sapling here, a yellow-staining stream of urine there. I catch its acrid musk before I see it on the snow.

Rabbits have wandered in the first light as if they were not still easy prey for the barred owls that live on the hill. Odd backward tracks seem to mislead. Which way did he go? They fool only unaccustomed humans. The owls are not deceived, nor do they track.

The owls have hunted well last night. I find the intersection of rabbit and owl beside the ice-glazed road. No tracks leave the killing ground. There are only the signs of a scuffle and of the long repast and a tuft of silly fur blowing in the wind.

FEBRUARY 6 · *Night*

The stars are tentative tonight, too shy to appear before such a cold audience. It is just above zero, and I came out to look for the evening paper in its blaze-orange wrapper. I was planning only a brief run and left my quilted coat hanging inside the door. But the stars that appear one by one in the deepening sky have caught me short, and I am a captive audience watching the light show. Three stars glitter in the sky when I first go out—stars that are not stars at all but planets—Mercury, Venus, Jupiter, the evening "stars" of a winter night. Then another light winks on, hanging there as if just beyond my reach.

It is in the constellation Orion. I recognize the position, if nothing more, just this side of the Dog star. I am the most amateur of astronomers and one with a most selective memory. I would not have known that much if I had not looked up this distinctive constellation again a few weeks ago.

As I watch, still more stars pop out as if from Pandora's box, barely visible in the opaque cobalt sky of evening. A ruddy flush still tints the west. Sunset is not far gone over the western ridge.

Finally, I count fourteen pinpoints of light where moments ago there were only three and among them are the three stars of Orion's belt. As the rest of this bow-tie formation takes shape, I head in. The scent of my own wood smoke on the air is as tantalizing as anything in this world tonight—with a more elemental appeal to a flawed and freezing human than the lovely stars in a cold night sky.

FEBRUARY 9 · *Night*

It is so dark this cloudy cold night that I cannot see my own feet. I cannot imagine how owls can see to find prey, but they do. The answer is in their specialized eyes, fine-tuned for night magic.

Those forward-facing eyes, so unsettlingly human in their straight-on placement, give owls greater binocular vision than any other bird. That is, out of a total field of vision of 110 degrees, the owl's eyes can take in 70 degrees of that total at one time. The binocular vision allows them to estimate distance and depth, essential to a predator. And although 110 degrees is not a very large range of vision, owls are able to turn their heads 180 degrees to see what they have missed. Behind them, if necessary.

One evening last summer as Harris and I walked the asphalt path at Watkins Mill we saw a strange owl, one that defied identification from familiar field marks. Its head was like our common barred owl, but the breast was far too dark. But it was not the breast at all. It was the big bird's back. He had turned his head completely around to observe us. In the thick foliage, I had been unable to see his stubby tail hiding his talons.

An owl's eyes are very big. They take up a large percentage of his face. They fit so tightly into their bony cavities that there is little room for controlling muscles; an owl cannot move his eyes about as we can. He has to move his head to see a larger range.

Unlike our round orbs, an owl's eyes are tubular, which further complicates the possibility of moving them within their sockets. They are longer than they are wide. But his corneas are big and his irises have a great range of expansion and contraction, which allows him to make extreme compensation for light levels. In the daytime, he can even lower his nictitating membrane to protect his eyes from too *much* light, as well as from physical damage. This membrane is much like that of my pet cats—thin and moist. But I usually see it on my cats when they are ill or sleepy. Owls use theirs constantly.

Nictitate means to wink, and that is essentially what this specialized wisp of tissue does. It allows the animal to close an eye at will and still see. Unlike us, he does not have to close up shop completely. Sight is still possible while winking. He blinks, but not totally, not unless he wills it.

An owl has a great expressive repertoire of ocular tricks. He blinks with his upper lid or his lower or with both at once. He can blink with the nictitating membrane alone or in concert with his lids. Like us, the owl may be capable of expanding and contracting the iris in reaction to emotion or interest or in response to distance and the need to focus, as well as to light conditions. The delicate musculature around his eye allows "expression" within the position of the surrounding feathers. So it is no wonder that an owl's eyes are considered hypnotic.

FEBRUARY 11 · *Evening*

A very urbane red fox stops rush hour traffic in its tracks at Forty-second and Main streets in Kansas City and scarcely looks anxious about his position—as if his own red light were sufficient to brake the cars. And so it is. Commuters stop to gawk like school children at the zoo.

As urbanized as this fox is, adapted to our ways and our presence, he is almost as domesticated as a zoo animal. Almost, but not quite. He dances around the edges of our civilization, dodging where he needs to to avoid contact, taking advantage of the food we inadvertently provide him, finding shelter where he can. Our city has become his territory, and it takes on a kind of wildness invisible to human eyes. Invisible, *usually*, until a brush-tailed fox darts between two lanes of traffic as if he were the true owner, the property holder—and he is. He holds the original land grant. We are the immigrants here.

FEBRUARY 13 · *Midnight*

The sound of melting is everywhere—a plop and trickle of sound, a liquid chuckle under the snow, a syncopated dance of droplets from the icicles that drip in the warm Chinook night. The midnight silence is populous with a matrix of auditory signals. Water impersonating life.

These rapid temperature rises are always a surprise. The Rocky Mountains, two states away, author the change. Air rising up the western slope cools rapidly; as it pours downslope on the east, it compresses adiabatically, five and a half degrees for every one thousand feet, speeding up like a freight train. The warming prevents further condensation, and the newly temperate air spreads out over the plains like warm syrup. We catch its mitigating exhalations nearly eight hundred miles away and bask in the Colorado Chinook.

FEBRUARY 15 · *Midnight*

The winter white weasel snakes across the snow, nearly invisible in this overcast night. His supple spine undulates like a cobra. He stops, sniffs the air and sits on his haunches with his front paws tucked up kangaroostyle. He is aware of each tick and trickle in the woods. His ears swivel and twitch, seismic receptors of each small sound. Hearing nothing threatening and intent on the scent of soft warm prey, he continues on his way, rocking over the rough terrain.

A great horned owl drops silently from the twisted limb of the red oak overhead. His primaries spread like fingers, their sound muffled by a fine fringe along each feather. As he nears the ground he brakes and swings his talons forward, then strikes. The weasel lets loose a high, quavering squeal as it rises helpless into the air. A trickle of red stains the white of his fur.

Helpless, but not so helpless, after all. He twists that supple spine, writhing in the owl's talons. He turns until he is within reach of the deeply feathered legs and sinks his small, sharp teeth into the owl's left leg. The owl reacts instantly. He drops the weasel before he has lifted him twenty feet in the air. The weasel hits the ground running. He may not be seriously hurt, only chastened. And out of there.

FEBRUARY 16 • *Sunset*

A winter sunset is alchemy of the most ancient order. All day the skeletons of weeds have stood gray and beige and brown. Broken, twisted, dry as death in the field, they are of interest only to the small flocking birds that find sustenance among the remaining seeds. But as night falls, and the sun drops below the day-long cloud cover to strike fire against the flint-hard earth, the weeds are etched in black and flame. Their fine, spidery lines are lace—a web of knots and arcs and wires. Their seeds and pods and spent flowers and small, dry bracts explode against the geometric web in a thousand lovely patterns, commanding our attention at last.

Suddenly, woven into the display that languished unnoticed in the daylight hours, there is graceful wild parsnip and finely carved Queen Anne's lace. Curled dock adds emphatic knotted lines, mooring the dark earth to the darkening sky. Ornate asters are there and fine-cut pineapple weed and rough blue vervain, a rococo chiaroscuro of lines and angles. Angelica explodes like fireworks, its umbeled head shot outwards in silhouette against the rose red sky. Milkweed pods swim through the woven net like graceful, turning fish, making good their endless escape.

Backlight has touched the ordinary with sudden magic, weaving an intricate web of night shadows. Not content with monotone black, lifeless, colorless black, the display is lit up against a field of blazing sunset. I would have driven right past it an hour earlier, never really seeing the mixed plant community that flourishes there.

FEBRUARY 17 • *Night*

I saw gnats about today and crocuses just testing the warming air with their pale yellow-green spikes. It must have gone to my head. I lit the porch light to see what flying insects might come to investigate. Will there be night gnats? Or moths? Or nothing at all. By 10:30 P.M. I turn off the light, all unvisited. It is still winter, after all.

FEBRUARY 18 • *Night*

Mitigating weather has brought flocks of Canada geese to Lake Jacomo in the next county. Is there a sign of spring more plain to decipher than those long arrows etched across the face of the moon, those high, wild voices that touch a place inside that has not been wild for a very long time?

The cardinals take to the high ground in the daytime, singing their fierce territorial anthems in the tops of the maples and sycamores. Crocuses poke their way through the hard ground. But the geese say spring with sounds I cannot ignore if I wanted to. We will have more cold, more snow, more freezing rain, but I can look through these small windows and see the turning of the year.

FEBRUARY 19 • *Dusk*

A walk into the sunset takes longer in these lengthening days. The sun, hidden all day behind fat cumulus clouds, stalls at setting. It peers out at last and sends fingers of light out to touch the hills that contain this small town. Warm light stains the pale gray limestone ridges that bridle the hills. It looks as though the color must remain when the sun is long gone. Far across the valley I can make out the far ridge in blue, deepening shadow. I walk the sunlit eastern ridge, blushing like the rocks, and marvel at evening just across the way, as if I looked into another time zone. My own house below is tucked into its pocket.

The twentieth century midden piles of trash catch the fading light. They demand our notice. Here, a white enamelled stove has been tossed out a back door and across the yard to tumble into a wooded ravine that could be lovely, if anyone cared. There, the pale shapes of polystyrene plastic and paper and the silver shine of beer cans swim like stationary fish down the limestone ridge that once marked the driftlines of a prehistoric inland sea. The gutters are full of our refuse.

Three hundred million years from now, will our trash turn to stone like the tiny fossils folded into the limestone? Will some geologist of the future wonder at their makeup, some archaeologist dig carefully to expose our midden and see how poorly we lived in this small town?

Like towns and cities of the Dark Ages, we live amid our garbage. We toss our trash from car windows and wallow in the detritus. It is a wonder we do not empty slop jars from upper-story windows and walk with kerchiefs held to our protesting nostrils.

The night at least will hide our trash piles. Let the encroaching inland seas of some millennia or another cover the evidence, bury it beneath the calciferous bodies of small marine animals. Have done with it. We will not clean up after ourselves.

FEBRUARY 20 · *11:30 P.M.*

The warmer daytime air has melted our snow cover in on itself. It is dense and crystal and now, when the temperature plummets, ice hard.

I step out to assess the night and find that my rude entry into alien territory (the night has other owners than myself) has frightened a family of raccoons dining beneath my bird feeder. They scatter, tripping and slipping and falling all over themselves to get away from my light. One splats to the ice on his belly in a perfect pratfall and just keeps skidding. Another tries to get purchase on the glaze and runs in place, a cartoon of motion. I expect a puff of smoke and a visible *zooom* when he finally makes good his getaway.

They are after the cracked corn the birds disdain. Used to finer things, the birds fling this plebeian fodder to the ground in contempt. There is a great gold mound of it insulating the snow just under the feeder.

FEBRUARY 21 · *Night*

The air is so warm it brings to mind hot buttered rum: smooth, soft, mellow.

The sky is lightly overcast and dark as a bat cave. Only one star is strong enough to shine through the invisible layer of clouds.

I step out from beneath the trees to try to find another star in this strange sky and nearly sink to my ankles in mud. On the farm, in mud time, we had to park at the top of our quarter-mile drive and walk out in the glittering dark each morning; it was impassable except on foot. If we were lucky, the night frost would firm it enough to walk on, if not to drive over. Tonight, this sucking, hungry mud reminds me of our sliding, sidewinding progress up our driveway to the car. I am glad I have only a few feet to walk these days.

FEBRUARY 23 · *10:15 P.M.*

The half-moon is nearly overhead, and Orion is already swept off to the southwest. The stars spin by with the seasons as well as with the hours. Their positions change nightly.

Closest to the moon, the stars are erased from the sky, crowded out by the light. There is a ring of them like a corona, as if flung out by centrifugal force. The Big Dipper seems to hang at the ready just over my sink as my grandfather's drinking gourd did.

It is as silent as ever I remember it at this hour, a silence that reaches within and searches each dark corner. Late winter thoughts sit in these corners, remembering, dreaming, speculating on what is what, and I luxuriate in the profound stillness.

On the evening news tonight, I find that the snowy owl is a minor celebrity. He is hundreds of miles south of his normal range, and the cameras catch him in midflight. Those big white wings beat the Midwestern air in slow motion as he searches the ground for something familiar—for prey. The light on his wings is blinding. This is one owl that hunts by day as well as by night. The camera has caught the truth of his hunt.

Joe Werner, the urban biologist, tells me that snowies have been found as far south as Oklahoma. But when they come this far from home range, they normally stay. The owl is alone here. There will be no breeding, no young.

FEBRUARY 25 • *Sunset*

As I sit soaking up the last of sunset's warmth—and the lovely silence—my nerves are rubbed suddenly raw by the sound of ATVs in the park. They come nearer and nearer, their noise a rising affront, an abomination, a violation of the peace.

Until the park department put up signs last fall, ATVs roared through the woods at will, running down wildflowers, upsetting the mating cycles of mammals and birds alike, leaving raw marks that bled topsoil with each rain—tearing up the delicate forest ecosystem. We very nearly lost the park's designation as a Missouri Natural Area when the Department of Conservation discovered the problem. Something had to be done to stop it, to repair the damage, and to protect the old-growth forest. New signs posted at the ATV-cut trails seemed to have stopped the incursion.

But now I am one ragged shard of anger, instantly on the defensive as I hear the rising whine of their engines. They are coming closer, crossing the creek, approaching the road that leads into the park. If they head into the natural area, now protected by law and new, posted signs, I will go for the police.

Such a law-abiding response. Go for the police. I want to puncture their tires, scream at them, shoot them, spike the trails, pick them off one by one, and watch them crash their idiot machines into a tree—if it could be done without damage to the tree.

Still, I sit at my place. My face registers nothing of the fury I feel. And inside I am murder incarnate. No wonder people are surprised when one of the quiet ones goes berserk, shooting off like Roman candles.

I love this place and its peace. I was instrumental in its recognition by the state and in its protection for future generations. And I am angry enough to protect it with violence—always a shock for a pacifist with limited self-knowledge. Perhaps I should find a way to convert this anger to energy. It would light the skies.

I will not shoot them, of course, nor will I spike the trails. As usual, calm and controlled, I will go for the police.

Weekends are not the time to go looking for peace in the park, at least before full dark.

FEBRUARY 26 • *Night*

The snow is gone except on the north face of Siloam Mountain; there it fluoresces blue in the darkness. The air is much cooler here than it is at home, refrigerated by that immense snowiness and the cold mineral springs that perforate the limestone.

At home, the longer days have triggered growth of crocus, tulips, and jonquils. The pale tips of the jonquils, bleached by the subsoil darkness to a tender yellow, are ghostly against the bare, muddy soil. I seem to smell spring in the air, a thin ectoplasmic scent that brushes against my cheek with a promise.

The earth must be aware of its coming. The trees respond to the RSVP with running sap. They will arrive on schedule at the edge of spring. The stumps of the maple we cut last fall glisten with the bodies of lined acrobatic ants, as they did the night we cut it. The ants are massed around a spot of damp on the largest stump. I taste it with a finger; it is faintly sweet. The sap has risen in this one small cut tree with no place to go, and the ants enjoy the bounty.

FEBRUARY 27 • *Sunset*

The rough pale grasses are a hundred delicate tints of wheat and ochre and gold. The wind blows them in long inland waves, and they break silently at the edge of the graveled road. But not quite silently. There is a muffled, rattling hiss like the sound of ocean waves on a protected sandspit.

We walk waist-deep across what was once meadow. It is now a part of Watkins Mill State Park. No farmer bales this tall grass. It is on its way to becoming forest. The open stretches are punctuated by aromatic cedars, dark silhouettes cut from paper and pasted on the ripe wheat-colored hill. Osage orange trees divide like cells from the edge of the meadow. Their young now scatter widely or gang up to form a daunting, impenetrable wall.

As we trudge through the eye-high skeletons of weeds, we scare up a coyote, and he does not catch our scent. We are downwind of him. He has not heard us, either, over the whine and blow and small clatter of the dry weeds. But at last he has seen us, turned tail, and absconded into the thick brush, silent as smoke. He pulls that wheat-colored, bottle-brush of a tail in after him.

These creatures are well adapted to our presence. We hardly know they are there, all around us, watching. Many interbreed with domestic dogs to form coy-dogs, and some biologists think the genuine article—a purebred coyote—is on the way to becoming as rare as virgin timber.

The old cemetery on the hill is suitably eerie. The wind moans and whoops and wails. The cedar, the oldest cedar of them all—it must be 150 years old, at least—stands above all the other trees like a fire tower in the little clearing. It is bleached a ghostly gray white, weathered, aged. Its limbs are broken and angular, but it is exuberantly, stubbornly alive in the spring-like wind; its dark green shape is visible for miles, like a signal.

At one time it had a double trunk. Half of it has died and has been cut back flush with the tree. Insects have tunneled deep into the dead wood, now barkless and cracked and as rough as a broken stump. This dead wood creaks and pops in the whine of the wind, rubbing somewhere deep inside against the living wood. It sounds like old bones in this ancient boneyard—the bones of the Revolutionary War soldier buried here. It is a strange place to be in the gathering dusk. Goose bumps rise on my arms. My hackles are deliciously up.

FEBRUARY 28 • *Twilight*

A small, ragged arrow of geese points silently to the sunset just passed. Not a sound hints at their passage. Noisy crows gather in small bands—a breeding pair and last year's young. They have just rejoined the resident birds, and the confrontation between migrants and residents is a cacophony of sound. Their return signals a completeness to the year and drops strong hints of spring.

Night is falling. It has gotten colder by the second. The gumbo track that spelled February mud time is hard enough to negotiate now if I step between the ice-skimmed puddles.

The light is blue and deepening rapidly as if we ourselves were fading. The earth is dark. But overhead, against a translucent sky, I see two moths flutter by, cold but moving. Their flight seems jerky, erratic, as if the cold had affected their trajectory. They are gone too quickly and fly too high to identify. And among all the choices of small, gray-brown moths, it would take an entomologist to call them by name. To me, their name is Spring. Ice on puddles notwithstanding.